HIDDEN HISTORY

of

JEFFERSON CITY

Michelle Brooks

THE
History
PRESS

Published by The History Press
Charleston, SC
www.historypress.com

Copyright © 2021 by Michelle Brooks
All rights reserved

Front cover: courtesy Cole County Historical Society.
Back cover, top: courtesy *Jefferson City News Tribune*; *bottom*: courtesy Nancy Arnold Thompson.

First published 2021

Manufactured in the United States

ISBN 9781467149419

Library of Congress Control Number: 2021937167

Notice: The information in this book is true and complete to the best of our knowledge. It is offered without guarantee on the part of the author or The History Press. The author and The History Press disclaim all liability in connection with the use of this book.

All rights reserved. No part of this book may be reproduced or transmitted in any form whatsoever without prior written permission from the publisher except in the case of brief quotations embodied in critical articles and reviews.

This book, Hidden History of Jefferson City, *might have remained hidden itself if not for the early encouragement of friends and family that this author was capable of the work. Three of those who championed the writing and the writer left this world too soon to see the final product.*

These pages are dedicated to Larry Dixon, cherished father, and inspirational coworkers Bob Watson and Shelley Gabert.

Contents

Preface	7
Acknowledgements	9
Author's Note	11
Part I. Origins	13
Chapter 1. Earliest Settlers	15
Chapter 2. General Assembly Arrives	22
Chapter 3. A German Influence	28
Part II. Media	37
Chapter 4. The First Printer	39
Chapter 5. The Lusk Newspaper Family	45
Chapter 6. Three Corwins Make Newspapers, Radio	50
Chapter 7. The Winter-Goshorn-Weldon Legacy	59
Part III. Moving Forward	67
Chapter 8. Crossing the River	69
Chapter 9. Mail and Hospitality	74
Chapter 10. Riding the Rails	82
Chapter 11. Breaking Barriers	89
Part IV. Building Up	95
Chapter 12. Defined by Water	97

Contents

Chapter 13. Gaining Power   104
Chapter 14. Crossing Bridges   113
Chapter 15. Lines of Communication   120

Part V. People and Places   127
Chapter 16. Bragg Hall, City Hall, Henry Bragg and
    Joseph Clarke   129
Chapter 17. Damels, Diggs and a Stone Testament   136
Chapter 18. Gentle Resiliency   141

Notes   147
Index   169
About the Author   175

Preface

This is not intended to be a comprehensive telling of the city's history, nor a timeline of events. I took the word *hidden* seriously in the assignment. My goal was to find lesser-known people, places and pillars of the Capital City's history.

Many intersecting stories I anticipate have been or will be told in works by other local authors, including Bob Priddy's history of the Capitol, Wayne Johnson's future work about people from Cote sans Dessein, Callaway County and Terry Rackers' book on the history of the local airport.

Since this year is the 200th anniversary of the Great State of Missouri and last year was the bicentennial for Cole County, it should be kept in mind that Jefferson City has its own bicentennials approaching.

My hope is that local history fans will still find in these pages those "I didn't know that" lines. And, perhaps, the reader lukewarm to the past will find a few pieces of history with which they can identify.

My dad loved science fiction. When *Star Wars* was released, I was a youngster. I remember asking him what it was about. He said it was a story following a pair of robots through the galaxy. Without having met the characters or learned the storyline, that answer did not really pique my interest. Then, we went to the theater. Except for crawling into my dad's lap at the first introduction of Darth Vader, I loved it. I understood what he meant about following R2-D2 and C-3PO through three generations of galactic unrest. But I also saw how they were just part of a greater story.

Preface

In writing this book on the hidden history of Jefferson City, I have looked at topics that might not sound glamorous or compelling on the surface. Utilities? Transportation? Media? Unless you're really into these things, they may sound superficially disinteresting. Please don't let that stop you!

Jefferson City's origin and growth has been dependent on its being the Capital City. That created challenges to achieve that purpose out of virgin forest and then to keep up with expectations as hundreds of legislators visited the city for only a few months every two years. Then, other cities wanted to take away the title and the heart of this central city. The race was on to build and become more than what the rest of the state might have thought of this rural town.

From the first newspaperman, innkeeper and merchant, strong, business-minded men and women have risked and sacrificed to develop a capital city for Missouri. Hoteliers made investments in buildings guaranteed to be filled for only four out of every twenty-four months. Ferrymen vied for control of the slim market of travelers crossing north to south on the Missouri River. Roads were carved after trees were pulled down and limestone cut.

The railroad brought an increase of visitors and potential, inspiring industry and diversified specialties. As modern innovations became available, men with families to provide for and their own businesses to maintain organized for the benefit not only of the city's future but also that of the state.

By the time of the second Capitol fire in 1911, Jefferson City's residents and business leaders had laid down the permanent lines of infrastructure. The decades-old criticism of Jefferson City being a backwater or unfit to remain the state's capital was put to rest in the statewide vote to rebuild the present Capitol building.

In this book are the stories of those builders, visionaries, risk-takers and entrepreneurs who laid the earliest and most essential foundations of the Capital City.

Acknowledgements

This book was not possible without the decades of work of historians who collected, wrote and preserved these stories. My biggest "thank you" has to go to newspapers as a whole. They preserve a world of history and culture and deserve our patronage as a looking glass for future generations. The filing cabinet on the west wall of the Missouri River Regional Library is a treasure-trove of clippings.

Reporters like Lawrence Lutkewitte took the time to talk with "old-timers" in his day to write a series of stories on local history in the 1940s. Other newspapers gave print space to visitors' recollections of their childhoods in the city and later to the Cole County Historical Society, whose members once contributed regular columns.

Local authors have published stories, including, Dr. Robert Young's "Pioneers of High, Water and Main," a phenomenal first-person recollection of the city in the 1840s and 1850s. There are also Dr. Walter Schroeder's first-person stories of Old Munichburg, local German community and the greater city's story.

Thank you to other custodians of local history, including Mark Schreiber, Gary Kremer, Henry Gensky, Nancy Arnold Thompson, Jenny Smith, Debbie Goldammer, Jane Beetem, Jeremy Amick, Arnold Parks and Craig Sturdevant.

My deepest appreciation goes to those who work at archive, museum and library settings for the valued impact of their preservation of and access to the pages of history. Specifically, Katherine Owens and John Petersen at

Acknowledgements

the Missouri State Museum were generous in their replies to my questions. Darrell Strope at the Cole County Historical Society was gracious with his time, allowing me to search the wonderful files in the genealogy library.

To the staff of the Missouri State Archive—you're the best! Christina Miller, Kelsey Berryhill, Ariadne Rehbein, Mary Mitchell, Daniel Reeder, Erika Woehlk, and others were easy to work with and knowledgeable of what materials the archive might have to help with specific queries. And thank you to State Archivist John Dougan for the casual chats that yielded Post-it Notes full of new sources to check out.

That gratitude extends to my coworkers in the imaging department for putting up with my random questions about local history and about their preferences in historic literature. Thanks to Taylor Allen, John Caples, Bridger Creed, Carl Haake, Joseph Hite, Lynn Voyles, Liana Twente and Kyrstin Keim. And to my boss and retired boss, Aaron Hodges and Bruce Meister, thanks for being flexible and supportive of my research!

Thank you to the people who were in the right place to help me fact-check or track down extra information, including Britt Smith and Pat Kliethermes at the City of Jefferson, Chip Webb at Ameren Missouri and Bob Priddy at First Christian Church.

For guidance and editing and for keeping me focused, thank you to Chad Rhoad, Rick Delaney, Madeleine Leroux and Randy Turner.

To everyone else who has encouraged me in this research and writing, thank you.

Author's Note

Most of the earliest settlers to mid-Missouri were from southern states. If they did not own slaves, they at least were comfortable with that culture. Enslaving other human beings was common in Jefferson City for its first forty years.

This book is not intended to glorify those who enslaved people.

The wealth of many of those who will be mentioned in this book was dependent on that institution. And many early building projects, no doubt, were possible only with the work of those in bondage.

Little history is recorded of the earliest African Americans in the Capital City. But their contributions are acknowledged by the author.

Here are a couple of examples of early African Americans, Luke Ferguson and Violet Ramsey.

Ferguson was the only African American listed on the 1840 U.S. Census in Cole County. He had been enslaved by Callaway County resident Joshua Ferguson, who built the first Callaway County Courthouse in 1826 in Fulton. When Joshua Ferguson died in 1834 at Cote Sans Dessein, he freed Luke, along with two other men, Adam and Ned; a boy, Bill; and a woman, Sally. In exchange, Luke and Ned were required "to cause Bill to be taught reading, writing and arithmetic at their cost and expense."

Ramsey received her manumission papers from Ephraim Clark in 1838 "for motives of benevolence and humanity," according to Nancy Arnold Thompson. She developed a highly successful washing business,

Author's Note

allowing her to buy several lots in town, including her home, where the predecessor of Quinn Chapel AME held its earliest services, and forty acres of farmland conveyed to Lincoln Institute in 1867. She also was able by 1845 to pay for the freedom of her husband, Elijah, and their youngest son, Elijah Jr.

Part I
ORIGINS

Jefferson City's existence is owed entirely to the state commission that selected the unclaimed, forested hills of limestone on the south bank of the Missouri River.[1]

The site of Jefferson City passed from Spanish to French hands, like all of Missouri, and then to the United States in the Louisiana Purchase. As the Missouri Territory, the site was part of St. Louis County, and then was included in the creation of Howard County in 1815. Three years later, it was part of the Cooper County split, and then Cole County was carved from that in 1820.

The state's earliest pioneers preferred the river bottoms and the richer soil of the north bank. The indigenous people, who predated the Osage and Missouri tribes back to the Mississippian prehistoric people, built burial mounds on the cliffs that would become part of the Capital City, including College Hill, today known as the Richmond Hill area, and the present Capitol Hill.[2]

The fate of this location might have been barren if one of the other, already populated sites—within the required forty miles of the mouth of the Osage River—had been selected by the commission. Howard's Bluff to the west was near Marion, the first settlement in Cole County, with pioneers arriving as early as 1816. Here, it was impossible to find the required 425 acres of unsold land, despite early residents' willingness to donate land.[3]

The prime contender was the French village of Cote Sans Dessein on the Callaway County side, east of Jefferson City. Trappers and fur traders were working out of that "hill without design" soon after the Lewis and Clark expedition passed by and a village formed by 1808. With about one hundred souls, it was the largest population center within the forty-mile range of the Osage River. To many of the legislators meeting at the temporary Capitol in St. Charles, Cote Sans Dessein was a done deal. However, land speculators and misused New Madrid earthquake land replacement certificates foiled the site's obvious selection.[4]

And so, Jefferson City—which might have been named Missouriopolis—became the "City a Capitol Built."[5] But, it is not the only state capital to emerge with an identity before residents arrived. Others include Columbia, South Carolina; Indianapolis, Indiana; Lincoln, Nebraska; Little Rock, Arkansas; and Madison, Wisconsin.[6]

Almost all of the earliest settlers to this area were of southern descent, and many were transplanted from either Marion or Cote Sans Dessein. Some of the richest men in the young state bought property early in the city's establishment. Within a decade, a second wave of influential settlers began to arrive: German immigrants.

And so, a few hundred men and women of vision took the dot on a map and built it into a capital city.

I
Earliest Settlers

Veterans of the Revolutionary War and the War of 1812 accounted for several of the earliest settlers in central Missouri. Rewarded with land warrants, they headed west, some stopping first in Kentucky and Tennessee.

Marion, near Howard's Bluff, on the south side of the Missouri River, and Cote Sans Dessein, a "hill without design" on the north side, were the two earliest population centers in the area. Between them, Revolutionary War veteran William Jones built a shanty on the south side of the river's edge, inside the future limits of Jefferson City, before 1819. Jones had joined the Patriot cause from Albemarle County, Virginia, during a draft of young men. He helped build huts in six-inch snow at Valley Forge, Pennsylvania, and then crossed the Potomac River to fight at the Battle of Monmouth with the Patriots.[7]

A future resident, James McHenry, remembered paying a silver quarter cut from a Mexican dollar for a half pint of liquor at Jones' shanty near a spring on what would become the west side of the Capitol. By the time Elias Barcroft arrived in 1822 to survey the future capital city, Cole County—organized in 1820—had licensed Jones to keep a ferry at Jefferson township.[8]

Jones served as one of the first justices of the peace for Jefferson City and was appointed an original city trustee when it was incorporated on November 7, 1825; he continued to keep his tavern. About 1829, William Jones moved to Rocheport when his son Robert took over the tavern. The younger Jones also served as city collector for six years and then moved his family to Texas.

Robert Jones married Mariah Ramsey, a daughter of one of the most prominent families in the area. Her father, Jonathan Ramsey, was brigadier general of the territorial militia and a state representative in 1820. Jefferson City, in part, owes its existence to Jonathan Ramsey. He is credited with including the Missouri General Assembly's limitation that the permanent seat of government be on the Missouri River within forty miles of the mouth of the Osage River. A resident of Cote Sans Dessein at the time, Ramsey likely was angling for his own home to receive the political designation.[9]

The first two hundred of one thousand original city lots were sold in May 1823.[10] By that time, Josiah Ramsey Jr., son of Jonathan and brother of Mariah, had moved to the south side of the river, making him the second resident of the future "Capital City." So, at the time of the first lot sales, the population included William and Mary Jones with their youngest children, John and Rebecca; Josiah and Martha Ramsey with son Lycurgus; and the enslaved people they brought with them.

The five commissioners appointed by the state general assembly—John Thornton (Howard County), Robert Watson (New Madrid County), John White (Pike County), James Logan (Wayne County) and Daniel Morgan Boone (who replaced his late brother Jesse B. Boone from Montgomery County)—gave their final approval of this bleak site as the permanent seat of government to the Missouri General Assembly on December 31, 1821, a year after being given the task. It met the required four sections, or 2,560 acres, of unclaimed public land, because, as the commission described, the land was "too poor to support any considerable population or extensive settlement."[11]

Soon after that decision, Major Elias Barcroft laid out one thousand one-half-acre in-lots and five forty-acre out-lots with the help of his wife's uncle Daniel Morgan Boone. Principal streets were measured between 100 to 120 feet wide and alleys 20 feet wide. The survey work took 120 days; the workers were each paid four dollars. A New Jersey native, Barcroft had been surveying land as early as 1808 in Ohio and then Illinois and had been appointed deputy surveyor of the Missouri Territory in 1813. He was responsible for surveying the Fifth Principal Meridian, which served as the baseline for future surveys of two million acres of land in the Louisiana Purchase.[12]

Barcroft, a senator for Howard and Cooper Counties when he did the survey, was appointed state auditor the next year, serving ten years. When the City of Jefferson was incorporated in November 1825, he was among the five first trustees. He served as commissioner of school lands and for building the 1840 county jail, at the southeast corner of Monroe and McCarty Streets. Barcroft further served two terms as city auditor and two as city assessor. His home, at the southeast corner of Main and Madison Streets, was used as the post office after his death from cholera in 1851.[13]

With the survey work complete, the next thing the future Capital City needed was a capitol building. The general assembly designated May 1823 for the sale of two hundred lots to fund the construction of the statehouse. The day would generate only about $6,500, or about one-fourth of the building costs.[14]

To oversee the lot sales, three trustees, who were each paid $100, were appointed: resident Josiah Ramsey Jr., future hotel operator John C. Gordon and Adam Hope. Duff Green was paid $16 to publish the sale of lots.[15]

Jane Ramsey Ewing—another daughter of Cote Sans Dessein's Jonathan Ramsey and sister to trustee Josiah Jr.—was paid ten dollars to paint the first city plat map, which was lost in the first statehouse fire in 1837. On a white canvas stretched across a twenty-by-thirty-foot wood frame, she painted Broadway red, other north–south streets green, cross streets blue and two hundred lot numbers black.[16]

General James L. Minor praised her as "one of our most distinguished and estimable ladies" in an 1876 address to the Missouri House of Representatives. As a teenager, Jane Ramsey Ewing had moved from Kentucky to Callaway County with her family about 1817. At age twenty-one, she married Robert Allen Ewing, a War of 1812 veteran, at her father's home. At the time she painted the map, Jane was caring for her first child, Missouri Jane.

The young Ewing family eventually bought a 1,200-acre farm on the south edge of the city. They also bought the northwest corner of Madison at High Streets, where the City Hotel stood before today's Central Trust Building. By 1829, Jane Ramsey Ewing's husband, Robert, was the oldest attorney in the city; he later served as a Cole County judge. Their sons, Henry and Ashley, each served in the state legislature.

On May 5, 1823, Jane Ramsey Ewing's giant map was set up on a cleared space, which would become Broadway. During the sale, she stood alongside her creation with a long pointer, indicating each lot as it was called by auctioneer Wyncoop Warner, who also was Callaway County sheriff at the time.

Warner's wife, Minerva, was another niece to commissioner and surveyor Daniel Morgan Boone. Born to Quakers in Virginia who moved to Ohio, Warner served three years during the War of 1812, eventually being promoted to captain in the Nineteenth Infantry by General Andrew Jackson at the Battle of New Orleans. The Warners followed the Boone family to Missouri in 1819. The iconic pioneer Daniel Boone lived his last years with the Warners, who employed someone to take him hunting. Their oldest son, Theodore, hid his apples and nuts in his great-grandfather's future coffin, which the elder kept under his bed.[17]

While Jane Ramsey Ewing held the pointer and Warner called the lots, Jesse Franklin Royston served as clerk to the trustees, receiving eighteen dollars. Royston, also a War of 1812 veteran, waited fourteen years for Congress to reimburse him eighty dollars for a horse he had lost while in service with mounted Kentucky volunteers. Royston became a local justice of the peace and an original trustee when Jefferson City was incorporated in 1825.[18]

Adam Hope, one of the three trustees of the city lots that day, was an attorney who had lived in Franklin and Columbia before moving to Callaway County about the time of the sale. Hope bought only one lot at the first sale, the northwest corner of Jefferson at High, which would become Central Hotel.[19]

In contrast, the third trustee for the seat of government at the first sale, John C. Gordon Jr., bought nineteen lots that day, many of them the valuable corner lots for the eventual blocks and streets, including the future site of his tavern and inn, the Rising Sun, at the southeast corner of Water and Madison.[20]

The son of another Revolutionary War veteran who settled in Cote Sans Dessein, Gordon was an early justice of the peace. And when the county government moved to Jefferson City in 1829, its first meeting was held in his house, at the northwest corner of Jackson at Capitol, where Buescher Funeral Home is today. Until a new county courthouse was built, the government rented space for a clerk's office at Gordon's home.[21]

Gordon's brother Alexander also bought four prominent corner lots in May 1823. Warner, the auctioneer, bought two lots. The first resident, William Jones, bought only one lot, at the southeast corner of Harrison at Water Streets. Trustee Josiah Ramsey Jr. bought ten lots that day, mostly in the 200 and 300 blocks of East High Street, plus a couple of choice corners in the future Millbottom area. And his father, Jonathan, bought fifteen.[22]

These men were among sixty investors who bought the first two hundred lots, the average price being $32.75. The purchaser needed to pay only one-third of their bid, the follow-up installments to be made in May and November 1824.

Boone County merchant Peter Bass bought the most single lots, twenty-three. Born in Maryland, Bass lived in Nashville, Tennessee, before moving his family to Boone County in 1819. The Peter Bass plantation, ten miles

The Virginia Hotel, built at the northwest corner of Jefferson and High Streets, was one of the earliest hotels. It was later renamed Central Hotel. *Courtesy the Missouri State Archive Bob Priddy Collection.*

southeast of Columbia, may best be remembered as the place where African American horse trainer Tom Bass learned the trade. Peter Bass had been part of the failed effort to entice the seat of government commission to select the Howard's Bluff site near Marion.[23] Bass later served as a permanent seat of government commissioner.[24]

James W. Moss, a land speculator from St. Louis, bought sixteen lots and lived here briefly.[25]

State representative Alfred Basye, on the other hand, initially bought fifteen lots and moved his family from Howard County to Jefferson City. He eventually bought the entire 400 block of East Capitol Avenue, where he built the first brick house in the city. Basye later bought sixteen lots from Bass, and he once owned all of College Hill, today known as Richmond Hill.[26] He also served as a seat of government commissioner and as postmaster.[27]

Another Revolutionary War veteran, Christopher Casey—namesake of the local Sons of the American Revolution chapter—bought the four lots on the north side of the 300 block of Miller Street.[28]

Daniel Colgan Jr., who would open the first general store in Jefferson City not long after this sale, bought one lot on the south side of the 100 block of East Main Street, where the First Presbyterian Church was built, and another at the northeast corner of Harrison at Main. Colgan had opened the first general store in Cote Sans Dessein in 1822 with his father, a tailor and former justice in St. Charles.[29] Colgan moved to the future Jefferson City site by November 1823, when Jefferson Township was established in Cole County after a meeting held at his house.[30]

Brothers McDaniel and Stephen Dorris each bought two lots, all on Water Street. Their father, an Irish minister, had been integral to the formation of the Baptist Cumberland Association in Tennessee. The Dorris brothers moved in 1818 to Callaway County, where Stephen Dorris served as a county court justice. After moving to Cole County, he served as a judge (the role held by commissioners today) and later was defeated for state senate.

Dr. Stephen Dorris began as a surgeon's mate in the Kentucky militia during the War of 1812. A town proverb in the mid-nineteenth century, "keep a-trotting," was attributed to Dr. Dorris. The story goes that in treating a patient in the last stages of consumption, Dr. Dorris asked him when he had felt the most relief. The patient replied, when he rode a hard-trotting horse. So, Dorriss' advice was to "keep a-trotting."[31]

The younger brother, McDaniel Dorris, set up the city's first distillery before the legislature arrived in 1826. His product was described as "clear and sparkling like spring water, with a potent quality that caused those who drank it to fight snakes where others could see no snakes," Dr. Robert Young recalled. In the 1840s, Dorris kept his whiskey at a saloon at 304 Madison Street.

By the Civil War, the Dorris distillery was located at the northwest corner of Lafayette and McCarty Streets. He also made peach brandy and applejack. Dr. Young said McDaniel Dorris would say his whiskey "was as innocent as the same quantity of buttermilk," yet it was also said, "if a man got drunk on it, it took a week to get sober again."[32]

McDaniel Dorris was described as having a "most happy disposition, always rendering him contented with himself and the world and thus no doubt greatly contributing to prolonged life.…He was distinguished for an uprightness and honesty which never suffered the slightest taint of blemish," his obituary in 1872 said. The only original pioneer to outlive McDaniel Dorris was Colonel Hiram Baber.[33]

Abraham Barnes bought the first lot recorded. Other investors in the first lots in the Capital City included the following: Peter Basye, Anson Bennett, John Brown, William Burch, John Burkett, Thomas Chews, Abraham Folia, Jacob Chisholm, Basman Clifton, Joseph Cooley, John Coonse, Cyrenius Cox, Solomon Craghead, Robert Dale, Thomas Daley,

Origins

James English, James Estes, Abram Foley, N.N. Foley, John Gibson, Jason Harrison, Hugh Harryman, Thomas Henry, Hiram Holt, Abner Holt, Eliza Hook, John Inglish, Samuel Jamison, William Lenox, Jonathan Martin, Henry May, Martha Ramsey, Robert Wash, Daniel Scrivner, J.B. Sexton, Leo Sexton, John Simonds Jr., Henry Sprinkle, William Tooms Jr., Andrew Walker, A.J. Williams, William Wilson, Jacob Zumwalt, Abram Zumwalt and Christ Zumwalt.[34]

2

GENERAL ASSEMBLY ARRIVES

By the time the Missouri General Assembly met for the first time on November 20, 1826, on the wilderness bluff where the statehouse had been built, entrepreneurs had been busy creating a habitable place for the future. Josiah Ramsey Jr., one of the first two residents of the site, was named the first postmaster in the summer of 1823. The township of Jefferson within Cole County was established that November.[35]

Development picked up after the general assembly awarded the construction contract for the first statehouse in February 1825 to Cote Sans Dessein entrepreneur Daniel Colgan. The two-story, sixty-by-forty-foot brick building, which faced north to the Missouri River, was required to have a rock foundation and eight fireplaces and be built on the west side of the 200 block of Madison Street, where the Executive Mansion is today. The project drew many new residents with building trades.[36]

Among them was James Dunnica, who took over the building contract from Colgan. Much of the city's early architecture can be attributed to Dunnica, including the first courthouse, located on the same site as today's courthouse, and the first county jail, at the southeast corner of Monroe and McCarty Streets.

Born in Kentucky, Dunnica was a tanner, shipping furs to St. Louis from Cote Sans Dessein when the Jefferson City opportunity arrived. While working on the statehouse construction, Dunnica also partnered with Calvin Gunn to establish the first newspaper in town, the *Jeffersonian Republican*; its office was across Madison Street.[37]

Later, Dunnica was appointed a commissioner to supervise the building of the Missouri State Penitentiary with a $25,000 appropriation from the 1833 general assembly. He was instrumental in bringing teacher George Wear Miller to town in 1827 and was a charter member and the first grand master of the Jefferson Lodge no. 43 Ancient Free and Accepted Masons.[38]

Carpenters who worked on the statehouse project included John Dunnica, John P. Thomas, Terry Skurlock, David Slater, Granville P. Thomas, Azariah Kennedy, Willis Thornton, David Harmon, William Henderson and Mr. Thompson. Specialists included blacksmith Hardin Casey, stonemasons Alexander Gordon and James R. Pullen and brickmason Reuben Garnett. Laborers David Scrivner and Samuel Harrison rounded out the crew.

The front of the statehouse faced north to the Missouri River. One half was used for senators on the first floor and representatives above. The other half served as the governor's residence. Bachelor John Miller was the first governor to take up the residence. A War of 1812 veteran from Howard County, Miller won the position in a special election in 1825 because Governor Frederick Bates had died in office in August 1825 and Lieutenant Governor Benjamin Reeves had resigned.

It was an awkward beginning. Visitor Ethelbert Lewis, in an 1837 letter home, said the strange gathering of "backwoodsmen and dandies" in the statehouse could be mistaken for a grog shop.[39]

In 1829, a kitchen, smokehouse and privy, all of brick, and a frame stable were added to the state grounds. Merchant Daniel Colgan's uncle Harvey Colgan built the first governor's residence in 1833 at the northwest corner of Madison at Main Streets, allowing the state auditor, library and secretary of state to occupy the second half of the 1826 statehouse. The first permanent Capitol was under construction in 1837, when the Colgan-Dunnica statehouse burned.[40]

When the Fourth General Assembly arrived with thirty-eight representatives and fourteen senators in November 1826, the city was filled with more than construction workers. And while history recorded only the names of heads of families at the time, at least fifty women and children lived in Jefferson City in 1826, in addition to the thirty named men.

In addition to newspaper editor Calvin Gunn, McDaniel Dorris had set up the first distillery. His brother Stephen was a doctor. Colgan had opened the first general store on what would be Capitol Hill, and Hardin Casey had opened a gristmill in the 100 block of East High Street.[41]

Jefferson T. Rogers had a tannery and ferry landing at the north end of Harrison Street. Christopher Casey was constable, and Robert A. Ewing was a lawyer. George Woodward and Robert Jones were merchants, Hiram Baber was a teacher and James Moss was a grocery keeper. Other residents at the time were Henry Buckner, a farmer, and Jesse Royston, who was a permanent seat of government trustee.[42]

The most notable of these earliest entrepreneurs is likely John C. Gordon Jr. When more than one hundred legislators and staff looked for accommodations, Gordon offered the only commercial hostelry during that first legislative session. Some visitors to the new village found boarding with residents, others in tents. Gordon's Rising Sun tavern and inn across Madison Street from the statehouse overlooked the Missouri River. The front entrance was decorated with a "picture of the sun in its meridian splendor, rays glowing, points glittering," the 1876 *State Journal* said.[43]

Gordon received a tavern license from the county government in advance of the legislators' arrival. Josiah Ramsey, Ralph Briscoe and Job Goodall received tavern licenses a few weeks later. But Gordon was the only one who also had an inn at this point.[44]

In June 1825, Gordon and Alfred Basye had made an agreement: Gordon would build for Basye a twenty-four-by-thirty-foot log house set on stone pillars in the 400 block of East Capitol Avenue, where Basye had built the first brick home in town. In exchange, Basye would give Gordon three lots of prime real estate at the intersection of Madison and High Streets and twenty thousand bricks by September 1826. Gordon used the bricks to build his hotel, a property that Basye would own later.[45]

As two of the greatest landowners at the time, obviously, Gordon and Basye had eyes on the future of this yet-to-be-built city, when it was just hills of ancient forest.

Gordon was the oldest son of Revolutionary War veteran John C. Gordon Sr., who moved from Virginia to Kentucky before settling at Cote Sans Dessein in Callaway County. While in Kentucky, Gordon Jr. married Cassandra Casey, the daughter of another Revolutionary War veteran, Lieutenant Christopher Columbus Casey. The Gordons and Caseys, including Christopher Casey's son Hardin and John Gordon Sr.'s son Alexander, settled in Cole County by 1823.[46]

The Gordon family home was at the northwest corner of Capitol and Jackson Streets, where Buescher Funeral Home is today. The first Cole County circuit court meeting in Jefferson City after the seat was moved from Marion in 1829 was held there. Office space was then rented temporarily in the home for the county clerk's office.[47]

The Caseys had come to Kentucky from South Carolina. In Cole County, Christopher Casey served as county coroner and is the namesake of the local Sons of the American Revolution chapter. His son, Hardin, built the county's first gristmill on the north side of the 100 block of East High Street. His brother and Revolutionary War veteran, William, also migrated to Cole County.[48]

Unlike the Kentucky soldiers, Basye came from a Virginia family of distinguished cousins, including two presidents and a U.S. Supreme Court judge. Basye arrived in Missouri before its statehood and represented Howard County while the temporary seat of government was in St. Charles. He built the first brick home in Jefferson City at 420 East Main Street and brought with him sixty cattle, twenty horses, thirty enslaved people and his own bricks made north of the river.[49]

Basye was a land commissioner and postmaster. His family continued to operate a boardinghouse at Gordon's Rising Sun location after Gordon sold in 1846. Following Basye's death, his daughter Susan continued to keep the hotel through the Civil War, when it was informally designated "Fort Jackson."[50]

After Missouri lawmakers decided to remain loyal to the Union in 1861, Governor Claiborne Jackson refused to provide troops; eventually, he and his Southern-sympathizing government were run out of the state, with the state seal in hand. Susan Basye's inn became the gathering point for Southern sympathizers in the Capital City on hearing of Jackson's defiance. According to the May 8, 1861 *Examiner*, a rebel flag—red and white striped with eight stars in an incomplete circle—was raised at the Basye Mansion.[51]

Behind the home, on the eastward slope parallel to Water Street, was a sizeable orchard. Despite her Southern leanings, Susan received help from General Ulysses Grant when Union soldiers were destroying the property during the Ffederal army's occupation of the capital city. Another time, when an intruder threatened the east end of the Basye property during the war, Susan Basye grabbed the family saber from over the mantel and chased him herself.[52]

Next door to the Rising Sun, George Miller taught school briefly before becoming postmaster in October 1829. The two-room log building he used as post office until 1841 sat on the south side of the 300 block of East High Street, across from the courthouse.[53]

Miller represented Cole County for two terms, then as senator for four terms, followed by elections to state auditor and attorney general. During the Civil War, he was the only circuit judge in the state never deterred from holding court.[54]

South of Miller's schoolroom was the offices of the *Jeffersonian Republican*. Editor Calvin Gunn moved his operation from St. Charles in pursuit of the lucrative state printing contracts. He built a temporary log home for his family near the northeast corner of Madison at Capitol.[55]

Several people from Marion moved to the Capital City, especially after the county seat was moved. The earliest settlement in Cole County was the Tennessee colony in 1818, which became Marion in 1820.[56] Joshua Chambers, who had operated a horse-powered mill in Marion, was one of the first to move to Jefferson City by 1826. In 1876, Chambers was the oldest remaining of the Tennessee colony settlers.[57]

Merchant Thomas Miller had one of the earliest marriages recorded in Cole County, to Margaret Kenyon. They were married by Justice of the Peace Thacker Vivion in July 1822. Miller, an original trustee for Jefferson City in 1825, was appointed as one of three agents assigned to get a loan for a new courthouse in 1836.[58]

Several of the builders of the first statehouse had moved on by the 1830 census. Carpenter Terry Scurlock was not one of them. Scurlock had served in the Tennessee militia during the War of 1812 and then signed up for five years in the U.S. Rifles Regiment, being discharged in 1819.[59] He continued to work as a carpenter in Jefferson City. Laborer Terry Scrivner, on the other hand, moved to the Russellville area, where he owned 240 acres.

The last of these original frontiersmen to settle in Jefferson City was Hiram Baber. Apparently, he was quite a character. He was described as a "reckless, fun-loving sort of a man." In St. Charles County, he served one term as sheriff. There, Baber had built a brick home, carving "Root Hog or Die" above his front door.

Not a miser, he was said to have lit his pipe with bank bills "in braggadocio…to show how easily he could make money and how little he cared for it." Baber was born in Virginia but reared in Kentucky. He arrived in St. Charles County by 1819, when he married Harriett Morgan Boone, another granddaughter of famed frontiersman Daniel Boone.[60]

Baber was active in the ginseng and pine trade through his St. Charles store. He was helped by his uncle-in-law Morgan Boone, who operated a sawmill in the Gasconade River basin, Missouri's largest ginseng region. Baber was the last living member of the state's first constitutional convention, held on June 12, 1820, in St. Louis.[61]

Harriett Boone Baber, like several sisters and cousins who also moved to Jefferson City, was the great-granddaughter of Squire Boone, who arrived at age twenty-one with the Society of Friends, immigrating from Devon, England, to Pennsylvania and later to North Carolina. Her middle name comes from the maiden name of her great-grandmother, Sarah Morgan.

ORIGINS

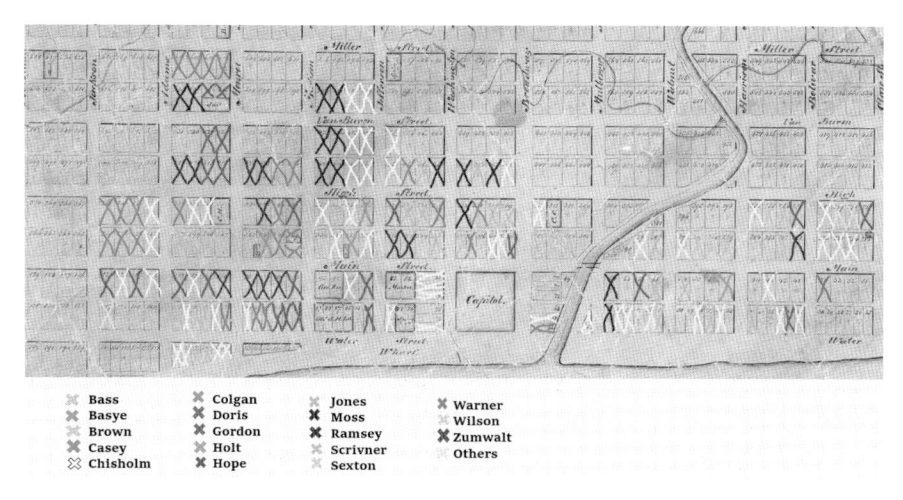

The first two hundred lots of the undeveloped Capital City were sold in May 1823. *Courtesy Missouri State Archive. Paint by Michelle Brooks.*

Her grandfather Daniel Boone continued from North Carolina to Kentucky in 1770. Harriett was an infant when her parents, Jesse and Chloe Boone, moved to the Spanish territory west of the Mississippi River after her grandfather received land grants in the future Missouri Territory.

Baber joined his brother-in-law Elias Barcroft, who had surveyed Jefferson City in 1822, in the state auditor's office about 1823 in St. Charles. Baber and Barcroft carried the state archives from St. Charles to Jefferson City by canoe along the Missouri River.[62] The first Cole County census in 1830—470 families, population 3,023—was recorded by Baber, who served eight years as state auditor and register of lands.

The earliest residents dedicated decades to improve the site, built from a raw frontier. But it would be nearly a century's legacy for city leaders to overcome the following sentiment, stated by engineer John Shriver, surveyor for the national highway from Wheeling, Virginia, to Jefferson City in 1829, and held by much of the rest of the state regarding the Capital City: "A rough looking city indeed, and one which does not bid fair to become of much importance."[63]

3
A German Influence

A wood joiner from Trier, Prussia, Josephi Wallendorf, and his wife, Elisabeth, boarded the ship *Georg Heinrich* at Bremen with their six children and arrived in New York on October 3, 1836. Like most early German immigrants to Missouri, the Wallendorfs likely were inspired by Gottfried Duden's 1829 book *Report on a Journey to the Western States of North America*.[64]

Duden had traveled from Europe with farm manager Ludwig Eversmann and their cook, Gertrude Obladen, settling in Montgomery County, later part of Warren County. The Wallendorfs likely followed the same path, west across the young nation, looking for a replica of the German landscape, free of squabbling politics and denominations competing for total control.

Set on the edge of the Ozark Mountains with plenty of available land nearby, the Capital City offered room and opportunity to the coming wave of German-speaking immigrants from many European provinces. The earliest German immigrants to Cole County arrived before 1840.[65]

The frugal, do-it-yourself culture was in contrast to the southern aristocracy ideal held by some of the earlier residents. These contrasting cultures would work together to build this city, though some issues, especially emancipation, would divide them.

The Wallendorfs likely arrived in Cole County about 1837, when they began homesteading on their first forty acres, which they bought following the five-year occupation period during early settlement. With Josephi Wallendorf's training as a carpenter and his five boys ages nine to twenty-one, the family's double-dogtrot log cabin would have been up in no time.[66]

The Wallendorf family was among the first of the German immigrants to settle in Jefferson City, building their double-dogtrot log cabin just southeast of town. *Courtesy Jane Beetem.*

As the city's limits grew, the Wallendorf homestead, in the area of Missouri 179 and Edgewood Drive, became part of the city. And as future development occurred, the cabin was preserved by relocating it a few miles farther west, at the Missouri Farm Bureau Agriculture and Rural Heritage Museum.[67]

Exceptionally large for the time it was built, the Wallendorf home was forty-two feet by twenty feet and two stories tall with a ten-foot-wide central hall. The home passed to son Bartholomew after Elisabeth's death in 1854. Family legend said it was the location, in the fall of 1864, where Confederate general Sterling Price made the decision to turn his invading troops west rather than attack the Capitol, where he had served as governor (1853–57).[68]

Devoted Catholics, the Wallendorfs originally were considered members of the Westphalia parish in Father Ferdinand Helias' list of parishioners compiled in 1838. That same year, Father Helias celebrated Mass in Jefferson City for the first time at the home of Henry and Gertrude Haar.[69]

The Haars had recently moved into Jefferson City from Haarville, originally the settlement Blocktown, in eastern Cole County.[70] They sold ten acres to Father Helias, who established his home and St. Francis Xavier parish. The community was finally named Taos after 1848 in honor of Cole County soldiers who had fought in the Mexican-American War.

While records say about 150 Catholic souls lived in Jefferson City about 1840, only nine private homes were registered. In addition to the incoming German immigrants, many of the Catholics at the time were Irish laborers who worked on the second Capitol.[71]

The first Mass in Jefferson City had been celebrated at a frame home at 327 West High Street in 1831 by Father Felix Verreydt, a Belgian Jesuit serving the Indian Mission at Portage des Sioux in St. Charles. A later brick addition to this house, known as the Upschulte House, was relocated and preserved behind the Cole County Historical Society.[72]

After the arrival of Helias, a Society of Jesus missionary, Catholic families in Jefferson City met monthly from 1838 to 1846. Although the Belgian priest never accomplished his dream of serving Native Americans, he instead is the namesake of Helias Catholic High School, in recognition of his tireless work establishing about twenty-five missions and parishes in the wilderness of central Missouri.[73]

Father Ferdinand Helias established many missions in central Missouri as a Jesuit missionary, including the one that became St. Peter Church. *Courtesy St. Francis Xavier Church, Taos.*

The early Catholic families in Jefferson City eventually raised $1,600 (equivalent to $44,700 in 2020) to erect the first Catholic church, in 1846. Land had been offered away from the downtown, but the parishioners were committed to a centralized location. Were it not for four "nay" votes in the Missouri House of Representatives, St. Peter Church might have stood on Madison Street, near where the Governor's Mansion is today.[74]

The first church was a modest log building facing High Street, about where the present St. Peter School is today, and was built with the aid of Capitol architect John Withnell and the other Capitol construction workers. Although Father Helias dedicated the work to St. Ignatius Loyola, Father James Murphy, who arrived in July 1846 as the first resident priest, dedicated the oak church to St. Peter as the fifty-ninth parish in the St. Louis diocese.[75]

Congregational leaders Bernard Eveler and Johan Bernard Wolters had been sent by the congregation to St. Louis to make the request for a full-

Origins

time priest. Wolters was one of the earliest German immigrants, arriving in Baltimore, Maryland, in 1836 from Hanover. A shoemaker, Wolters married Elisabeth Ahrens, a weaver, who had arrived on the same ship, the *Ulysses*. Wolters became a successful merchant, accumulating more than $33,000 (equivalent to more than $1 million today) in real and personal estate within twenty years.

A farmer and builder, Eveler and his wife, Margaretha, built the pre–Civil War Stone House at 728 West Main Street on College Hill, today known as Richmond Hill. The traditional, six-room home featured the double front doors of the German American vernacular and served as a landmark for travelers entering the Capital City from the west. During the Civil War, it was used as the gatehouse to the Union's Fort College Hill, which extended from Bolivar Street west past today's water tower overlooking the river.[76]

One block east toward the Capitol from the Evelers, Henry Haar's brother Herman, also a builder and a brickmason, built a home nearly identical in size and style in brick around 1859 at 614 West Main. Stephen Bergman, a Prussian millwright, bought the home in 1865, and it stayed in his family until 1944.[77] The building, with a double-front door, was relocated in 1986 around the corner to 110 Bolivar Street.

The Haar brothers built many of the earliest homes and businesses in the Millbottom–Richmond Hill, as well as the stone foundation for the second

The Byrd-Haar-Bergman home was built at 614 West Main Street just before the Civil War by Henry Haar. *Photo from Library of Congress Historic American Buildings Survey Collection.*

St. Peter Church. Herman Haar lived across High Street from the church, where the Truman State Office Building is today. He built several homes along that block.[78]

The German influence in Jefferson City is evidenced in the prolific construction of brick buildings. There were so many early immigrants who were skilled tradesmen, stonemasons, brickmasons and carpenters. In fact, at one point, a city ordinance was passed requiring brick construction.[79]

Naturalizations were granted only after a minimum of five years of residency. Fleeing the strife of their European homeland, hundreds of German-speaking families made their way to central Missouri before the Civil War. Their origins included Prussia, Bavaria, Hanover, Alsace-Lorraine and Austria.[80]

From 1834 to 1900, 814 immigrations were naturalized in Cole County. The most came from Bavaria (193), followed by Prussia (129), then Hanover (90) and Austria (29). Another 62 came from Wurtemberg, Hesse-Darmstadt, Baden, Hesse-Cassel, Saxony, Sachs-Weimar, Bremen, Lichtenstein, Holstein, Oldenburg and Reuss.[81]

Of the other 190 immigrants naturalized in Cole County, 59 were Irish, 48 claimed Great Britain, 24 were from France, 19 from Holland, 18 from Switzerland and 14 from Belgium. The remainder came from Sweden, Denmark, Lombardy, Russia, England, Scotland, Hungary, San Marino and Canada.[82]

John Henry Sandfort, Adolphus Schenler and Peter Ferdinand Clarenbach all arrived in Missouri from Prussia in July 1834 through Baltimore, Maryland, along with fellow Prussian Charles E. Miller. They were the first German immigrants naturalized in Cole County.[83]

A handful of other Germans lived in Jefferson City by 1840, including Johann Philip Magerlee from Wurtemberg. Magerlee and his first wife arrived in New Bedford, Massachusetts, from Rotterdam in 1832 with his brother and sister-in-law. A saddler by trade, he had moved to Jefferson City by 1839, when he built a brick shop and home at 118 East High Street. He lost his property in 1846, unable to repay a loan. And by 1853, he had moved his family to San Joaquin, California.[84]

Watchmaker August Wilke also arrived in Jefferson City before 1840, when he married Doshe Miller. Naturalized in 1843, Wilke and two young daughters died in 1844. Like many of the earliest pioneers of the city, they are buried at Woodland–Old City Cemetery.

Perhaps the most successful of the earliest German immigrants was Gerhart Herman Dulle, a Hanoverian teenager who arrived in Jefferson

Origins

The Dulle Milling Company in the 400 block of West Main Street specialized in flour. *Courtesy Cole County Historical Society.*

City in 1838. He had "fixed habits of industry and frugality…of pleasing address and kindly nature," the *Jefferson City Daily Tribune* said. Dulle worked his way from a hod carrier (one who supports a bricklayer) to furnishing wood for the prison to brick manufacturing and mill operation. At the same time, Dulle established an expansive farm and dairy.[85]

In 1846, Dulle purchased the city's first steam mill, built in 1844 on Jefferson Street between Main and Water by Mr. Mitchell. Less than a decade later, he built a two-story steam mill in the Goose Bottoms, later known as the Millbottom. This building on the southwest corner of Main and Walnut was replaced in 1870 with the four-story Capitol Star Mill. It had a capacity of three hundred barrels of flour per day. Later, he added Victoria Mill on the north side of Main Street. Through these mills, loaded conveniently on to trains nearby, mid-Missouri crops crossed the nation through the beginning of the twentieth century.[86]

In 1858, Dulle built a two-story, four-chimney brick home atop one of the highest points in the county, overlooking the fledgling Capitol from the south. The home remains today on the original site of St. Mary's Boulevard and is still owned by Dulle's descendants.

When Major General John Frémont arrived in Jefferson City on September 26, 1861, in charge of the Union occupation, he took over the Dulle home as his headquarters, and Camp Lillie, named for his daughter, spread a sea of army tents southwest across the family farm. When the Confederate army, led by General Sterling Price, threatened to attack the city in 1864, family legend says the Union soldiers marched in a circle up and down the hill to give the impression their numbers were greater than they really were.[87]

Dulle helped many friends and relatives immigrate to Jefferson City, not only making the arrangements but also paying expenses. A kind and generous gentleman, he saw the investment as a means of developing the Capital City.[88]

Many of these pre-1840 German immigrants were craftsmen and had a hand in building the earliest state buildings.

Christopher Kolkmeyer laid the first stone for the 1837 Capitol. He and his brother Frederick were stonemasons from Hanover. The Kolkmeyers lived in the Goose Bottoms area and operated a quarry near where the Missouri State Archive is today. The facility served their prosperous street and gutter work.[89]

Josephi Wallendorf's son Mathias took the skills he learned from his father and built the first privy on Capitol Hill and the fencing for the Capitol grounds. Mathias Wallendorf owned a carpentry business and operated a sawmill in the Goose Bottoms at the north end of Mulberry Street.[90]

Hanoverian Herman Tellman was a blacksmith and locksmith working on the second Capitol and installing the locks on the first Executive Mansion. Tellman, who fought in the Prussian army at the Battle of Waterloo, also helped build the first St. Peter Church, putting up the iron cross on the log building.[91]

Most of the earliest German immigrants were Catholic. Later, a strong Lutheran and Protestant contingent would arrive, helping establish today's Central United Church of Christ and then Trinity Lutheran Church. And a handful of early German-speaking merchants and residents were Jewish, being among the founders of Temple Beth El, today the oldest synagogue building west of the Mississippi River still in use and the fourteenth oldest in the country.[92]

The Bavarian Obermayer brothers provided the impetus for the Jefferson City Hebrew Cemetery Association to organize, creating the Maple Grove

Origins

Jewish Cemetery in the 1300 block of East McCarty Street, as well as Congregation Beth El in 1883.[93]

The oldest brother, Louis, had died during the 1849 cholera epidemic and had to be taken to St. Louis for a proper Jewish burial. When Moritz Obermayer died in 1876, he was buried with his brother at New Mount Sinai Cemetery in St. Louis.

The Obermayers learned weaving and the merchant trade from their father. After arriving in Jefferson City, they opened a mercantile at the northeast corner of Madison and High Streets. It was the oldest business in town by 1877. Simon, the first to immigrate, and Louis operated the store, while Joseph and Moritz made caps, which they also sold.[94]

Another pre-1840s influential German-speaking family, the Maus siblings were the children of a Lutheran minister who fled Hesse in 1829. Their father drowned soon after their arrival in Pennsylvania, and the mother died just a few years later, after moving the family to Ohio. By that time, the eldest sister, Elisabeth, had married Peter Miller, who also came from their hometown of Michelstadt.[95]

Elisabeth and Peter Miller moved to Jefferson City about 1839 with her four younger brothers, Jacob, Killian, Charles and Christopher, three being teenagers at the time. Jacob Maus worked as a merchant to support his family. Charles and Christopher learned the building trades. While Charles served in the Mexican-American War, Christopher joined the 1849 gold rush to California. Both returned to Jefferson City, where their older brothers, Frederick and George, also had settled.

In 1852, Charles Maus and his brother-in-law Charles Lohman bought the east section of James Crump's Missouri House, built in 1839 at the southwest corner of Jefferson and Water Streets. It is today one of the oldest commercial buildings in town, preserved at Jefferson Landing State Historic Site and commonly known as Lohman's Landing.

In 1855, Charles Maus built the Missouri Hotel, at the southeast corner of Jefferson and Water. After his first wife's death, his business partnership with Lohman dissolved in 1859, but he was joined in the hotel and grocery business by his brother Christopher and their brother-in-law Peter Miller. Christopher built the two-story brick home south of the stone business house, today known as the Union Hotel; both still stand today.[96]

During the Civil War, like members of many Missouri families, Jacob joined the Confederacy, while George, Charles and Christopher served in the Union army. Frederick was killed during the war, when a spooked horse pulled his carriage in front of a train near Centertown.

Christopher Maus built this home in the 100 block of Jefferson Street. *Courtesy of the Missouri State Archive Summers Collection.*

After the war, Jacob, Killian and Christopher moved to Vernon County. But Charles Maus returned to his hotel, renaming it the Union Hotel. By 1870, he had closed the hotel business and was operating a forwarding and commission business for the railroad, as well as dry goods, grocery and hardware retail out of the riverfront location.[97]

By 1873, he had renovated the building at the northeast corner of Jefferson and High Streets, where he and his family lived above his dry goods business.[98] Wealthy by the end of his life, Charles Maus, who was a charter member of what is today's Central United Church of Christ, donated property for the Christian Science Church in the 400 block of Monroe Street.[99]

Many more German-speaking immigrants followed these early pioneers and made their own contributions to the city's growth, serving as business, political and faith leaders and creating a new dimension of the Capital City's young identity.

PART II
MEDIA

ONE OF THE KEYS to the American governmental system working for the people is the Fourth Estate keeping watch over the official three. However, to do that, the early one-man print shops, especially in the frontier, had to turn a profit, too. With bureaucracy needing its paperwork, a reliable state printing contract was necessary.

Not surprising, then, that, along with the builders, land speculators and merchants, there would be a newspaper. But not just one. In the 1800s, newspapers were unashamedly for one party or candidate. Their editorials and coverage could have a very sharp edge. Therefore, as political majorities in the statehouse shifted after an election, so could the appointment of the state printer.

The first government printer in Missouri was Joseph Charless, an Irish immigrant enticed from Kentucky to St. Louis by territorial governor Meriwether Lewis to publish the territorial laws and documents. The first *Missouri Gazette*, also the first newspaper west of the Mississippi River, was published in July 1808.[100]

The first newspaper published west of St. Louis was Nathaniel Patten and Benjamin Holliday's *Missouri Intelligencer and Boon's Lick Advertiser* out of Franklin in April 1819.[101]

In Jefferson City, the first newspaper was Calvin Gunn's *Jeffersonian Republican* in 1826, in advance of the first meeting of the general assembly in the new statehouse, appropriately across Madison Street from Gunn's printshop and next door to John C. Gordon's tavern and hotel.[102]

The first competition in Jefferson City journalism came in 1838, when E.L. Edwards and John McCulloch opened the *Jefferson Enquirer*, which passed to the Lusk family in 1840.[103]

After that, the *Metropolitan* opened in 1846, followed by the *Examiner* (1854), the *State Times* (1862), the *People's Tribune* (1865, from which today's *Jefferson City News Tribune* draws its business lineage), the *Daily Tribune* (1871), the *Missouri Volksfreund* (1876), the *Staatszeitung* and the *Daily Eclipse* (1878), the *Cole County Democrat* (1884), *Jefferson City Courier* (1894), *Cole County Rustler*

(1897), the *Daily Post* (1903), the *Daily Democrat Tribune* and the *Daily Capitol News* (1910) and *Mosby's Missouri Message* (1918).

Robert C. Goshorn consolidated the last of the newspapers into a monopoly in 1932, although he retained a morning Democratic edition and an afternoon Republican through the 1950s. Goshorn also introduced the first commercial radio station to the city, KWOS. His daughter Betty Weldon became the third generation to continue the family legacy into the twenty-first century, and she became the first woman in the nation to open a television station, KRCG.

4
THE FIRST PRINTER

Orphaned and sent to a printer for his apprenticeship in Massachusetts, Calvin Gunn was a young print pioneer when he arrived in St. Charles before Missouri was a state. Gunn was awarded printing equipment in a lawsuit there and began printing for the new state's legislature while it met temporarily in St. Charles.[104]

As early as February 1825, Gunn had his eye on moving his printshop to Jefferson City and owning the state newspaper. He first proposed calling it the *Jefferson Patriot*. That fall, he opened the *Jeffersonian* newspaper in St. Charles.[105]

In advance of the first general assembly meeting in Jefferson City in November 1826, Gunn published the first five-column, four-page edition of the weekly *Jeffersonian* from Jefferson City on June 14, 1826.[106]

Gunn, age twenty-eight, partnered with a young and ambitious store clerk named William F. Dunnica. The latter, only nineteen at the time, had worked for Anson Bennett's mercantile in Cote Sans Dessein for two years. The arrival of the legislature and the newspaper partnership drew him to the south side of the river. After eighteen months in the print business, Dunnica moved into the state auditor's office as clerk.[107]

Although the name of James Dunnica, a builder, appears more frequently in Jefferson City's history, it is worth noting the success of a teenager taking a business risk and turning it into a stepping-stone for a career of "intelligent industry and frugality" in the early days of the Capital City.[108]

William F. Dunnica arrived at the Callaway County French village of Cote Sans Dessein at age eleven aboard a keelboat of Kentucky goods floated by his father, William H., in 1818. The patriarch died four years later, and William F. returned to Kentucky for better education. After his return to Cote Sans Dessein and Jefferson City, Dunnica became a St. Louis banker and then bought the land for and established the town of Glasgow in Howard County.[109]

When Dunnica left the newspaper, Gunn changed its name to the *Jeffersonian Republican*. Gunn's early editions reflected his focus on the state legislature. Other state, national and international news was the second priority, but the content was old, as it depended on the arrival of St. Louis newspapers by boat or horseback.[110]

Calvin Gunn moved his newspaper operation from St. Charles to Jefferson City in advance of the Missouri General Assembly's first session in the Capital City in November 1826. *Courtesy the Cole County Historical Society.*

At the time, the village that would become Jefferson City had little more than one hundred people. Local news received little attention. Even the first murder, occurring inside the prison, received only one paragraph.

Gunn built the city's first newspaper office conveniently across Madison Street from the first statehouse. The one-story, two-room building at 103 Madison, now the parking lot for Ameren Missouri, held two hand presses and other early printshop materials.

That block was the first to develop, in preparation for the Missouri General Assembly's arrival. North of Gunn's shop was John C. Gordon Jr.'s tavern and inn, called the Rising Sun. And south of his shop, also on the east side, was a stone storehouse owned by Israel Read, who had been wounded with a Pennsylvania militia at the War of 1812 Battle of Mississiniwa before opening his mercantile business in Jefferson City. Read was one of the most prolific landholders in the early city, owning as much as $30,000 in real estate (that's $865,000 in 2020).[111]

For his family, Gunn built a log home near the northeast corner of Madison and Main Streets. By 1833, the Gunn family was more comfortably accommodated in a double log home at 109 Madison, where the Cole County Historical Society is today.[112]

Media

The brick building at the northeast corner of Madison and Main Streets first held the newspaper office of Calvin Gunn's *Jeffersonian Republican*. *Courtesy Cole County Historical Society.*

In 1837, Gunn bought the adjacent, two-story brick tenement at 111–113 Madison from Reuben Garnett and then the prominent lot at the northeast corner of Madison and Main. Gunn paid Garnett, a Kentucky brickmason, to build a three-story, brick newspaper house there. Today, 205 East Capitol Avenue is one of the oldest structures in town and is occupied by the Missouri Petroleum Marketers.[113]

Another War of 1812 veteran, Garnett served in the Kentucky militia. He arrived in Jefferson City about 1833, married four times and had at least fourteen children. By 1844, he had moved from Jefferson City to a farm in Marion, which became one of the most developed in the county. He built many of the earliest brick structures in town, predating the influx of German masons.[114]

From his printshop, Gunn had a monopoly on both the city's news and the state printing contracts for more than a decade. As the first state printer, Gunn published the official minutes of the general assembly, laws of the state and federal governments and other government information.[115]

Other printers in the state also bid for this lucrative, reliable contract. But early on, Gunn's proximity gave him the edge. In 1826, Charles Keemle of the *St. Louis Enquirer* made a lower bid, but the committee on printing noted that it "is most convenient" to have the printer near the secretary of state for review. In 1828, Gunn's bid was approved over that of James H. Birch, who in 1827 had opened the *Western Monitor* in Fayette, becoming the westernmost publisher in the nation.

As with all newspapers of that day, Gunn was opinionated, supporting President Andrew Jackson and opposing Henry Clay and the Whigs. By 1833, Gunn had four competitors for the state printing. Again, his bid, though not the lowest, was selected, because the

> *"committee conceive it all important that the public printing should not only be done as soon as practicable for distribution, but in a proper and correct manner. Therefore, they are of opinion that this object can be accomplished more perfectly by having the work done here under the immediate inspection and superintendence of the Secretary of State where the printer and he could act jointly and as often as occasion may require. This can be done by getting Mr. Gunn to do the work. Whereas, if the printing is distributed out among many printers, it must necessarily not only produce delay and inaccuracy, but also augment the expenses of printing,"* Rep. David Sterigere reported.[116]
>
> *The committee "further observe that the public printing done by Calvin Gunn immediately after the adjournment of the last session for the General Assembly was done better, and in a shorter time than in any instance heretofore coming under their knowledge. Upon the whole they are all entirely satisfied that the work can be done cheaper and more accurately and much sooner by accepting the proposals of Calvin Gunn than any other printer and that the people can get the laws and journals much sooner in this way than any other."*[117]

The state's printing jobs were divided in the 1836–37 session, when Gunn received contracts only for the session's laws and joint resolutions and other smaller jobs. Chambers and Harris, from the *St. Louis Republic*, received the house and senate journals' work.

The first local news competition for Gunn arrived in 1838, when E.L. Edwards opened the *Jefferson Inquirer*. In 1840, that same competition, then in the hands of William Lusk, also competed for the state contract, splitting the work with Gunn during the next three sessions. Gunn's last year of state printing was 1848, when he was awarded both the house and senate journals. During most of this time, Gunn also received the federal government printing jobs.[118]

Media

In 1846, Gunn was elected Jefferson City's fifth mayor, being particularly concerned about the city's debt reaching nearly $2,000 at the time.[119]

About 1850, he suffered paralysis, attributed to working in the print environment, which kept him bedfast until his death in 1861.[120]

Gunn had accumulated quite a bit of property during his decades in the growing city. However, he died with few assets. He left his widow, Elizabeth, to operate a boardinghouse and manage the family's other properties, including a twenty-acre quarry between the Missouri State Penitentiary and the Lincoln Institute. Before the state dug its own quarry, much of the stone used in early government construction came from the Gunn quarry, including that for early prison buildings and walls.[121]

Elizabeth Gunn was a woman of kind actions and a devoted member of the Presbyterian Church. Her funeral was the last public event held at the first Executive Mansion, near the northwest corner of Capitol and Madison, before it was torn down in October 1871.[122]

In an instance of awkward timing, Elizabeth's son-in-law and executor of her estate also was the sitting governor. Governor B. Gratz Brown had married a teenaged Mary Gunn in 1858 after meeting her when he was a thirty-something representative. He had also been a newspaperman before he entered politics. The couple had spent 1863–67 in Washington, D.C., while he was a U.S. senator.[123]

Brown's election as governor in 1870 allowed Mary to return to her hometown. However, the old Executive Mansion was in such poor shape that she did not live in it. Instead, the governor and first lady stayed across the street

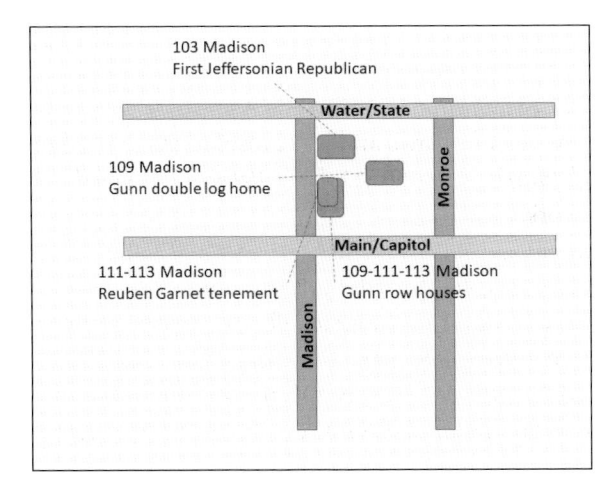

Map of locations associated with Calvin Gunn. *Michelle Brooks.*

from the old mansion in one of the new row houses built by her mother until the present Governor's Mansion was completed in January 1872.

The Gunns' Federal-style, three-story brick row houses at 109–11–13 Madison Street were designed by St. Louis architect John Ingham Barnett, also architect of the new Executive Mansion.[124]

In 1873, Governor Brown had to address the legislature on behalf of his mother-in-law's estate. The Gunn quarry had unresolved accounts with the prison. While wardens had sent inmates to quarry rock from Mrs. Gunn's property, they had failed to make settlement with her. The exchange of labor to help on projects for Mrs. Gunn and the removal of rock for construction had not been written down over the years, and wardens had changed.[125]

Although few editions of the earliest *Jeffersonian Republican* remain, Calvin Gunn's name is found on the title page of dozens of state journals and reports. And his vision of a strong Capital City is reflected in the row houses and the newspaper office that still stand on Madison Street, as well as the distinctive limestone from his quarry holding up some of the oldest remaining structures in town.

5
THE LUSK NEWSPAPER FAMILY

A man who would attempt to cheat a printer would refuse to pay for a coffin for one of his family. Them's our sentiments.
—*Lusk printers, 1846*[126]

The second newspaper established in Jefferson City was the third-oldest newspaper in the state when it closed at the dawn of the Civil War. The *Jefferson Inquirer* was opened by E.L. Edwards and John McCullough in 1838 to support the Democratic Party through the election. In 1840, it was sold to the Lusks, a Pennsylvania family that would build an admirable reputation for the publication before its end.[127]

E.L. Edwards moved from Tennessee to Jefferson City in 1831 as a teenager to study law with his brother John C., who just had been appointed secretary of state. After being licensed to practice law, Edwards was the first to hold the position of circuit court and county court clerk. After his two years in newspapers, Edwards worked as an attorney, being elected state representative during his brother's term as governor, and later as state senator.[128]

Edwards returned to newspapers in 1860, again because of the political issues and not as a profession. He served as editor-in-chief of the *Examiner*, an outspoken and well-known Democratic paper owned by W.G. Cheney that had the state printing contract at the time. He was in the unique position of competing with the newspaper he had started, still owned by the Lusk family.[129]

Pennsylvanian William Lusk settled on a farm eight miles west of Marion, now in Moniteau County, in 1839.[130] When he took over the *Jefferson Inquirer* a year later, he moved his family of Irish descent to Jefferson City, one of the rare early pioneers of neither German nor southern heritage.

Active in Whig politics in Pennsylvania, Lusk was a civil engineer, "endowed with energy and enterprise combined with perseverance and great mental determination," Goodspeed's 1889 *History of Cole County* said. After serving in the War of 1812, including at the Battle of Lundy's Lane, William Lusk was a music teacher and elected auditor and school inspector.[131]

The elder Lusk operated the newspaper for four years, until his death. At age twenty-three, James Lusk took up the family business, where he had been apprenticed. He was thrown into a situation of great responsibility, requiring mental and writing qualities that had been cultivated by his mother, Mary Fitzsimmons, through character-building and continual advice.[132]

James Lusk earned the contract to print the state's journals and papers in 1845 but was outbid in 1847 by Hampton L. Boone, editor of the local *Metropolitan*. Other papers across the state accused Jefferson City publishers of being "so desirous of securing the public printing that they are afraid to expose the sins of the members of the legislature," the *Boonville Commercial Bulletin* printed.[133]

When the *Jefferson Inquirer* was renamed public printer in March 1849, it was one of the more exciting matters of that general assembly. The Capitol lobby was crowded with ladies and gentlemen eager for the result. "Thunderings of applause from all parts of the hall" were heard when James Lusk was announced over Boone.[134]

To retain the title of public printer in 1853, the matter had to be considered by the Missouri Supreme Court. In the winter of 1852–53, the legislature failed to elect a public printer. Since James Lusk had been elected in February 1851, he should have remained, like the law said, "until his successor is elected and qualified."[135]

However, Governor Sterling Price appointed the *Jefferson Examiner* as public printer. The political play was to help in Price's campaign for U.S. Senate, editor John G. Treadway supporting Price and Lusk supporting the incumbent Thomas Hart Benton. The *St. Louis Globe-Democrat* said, "it was found by experience that abuse of Benton was a diet on which a paper could not live long in Jefferson City."[136]

Because of Lusk's position as a Benton Democrat—pro-Union and anti-emancipation—his position on slavery was questioned by both extremes.

That caused him to lose the public printer title to the *Jefferson Examiner* again in 1857.[137]

James Lusk was known as courteous, dignified and highly esteemed. He was an early vice-president of the State Historical Society and was the first Noble Grand of the Capitol Lodge no. 37 of the Independent Order of Odd Fellows.[138] Yet, a Pennsylvanian with northern views in a southern-leaning frontier town was not without troubles.

On the post office steps, at the northeast corner of Capitol at Madison, in June 1853, James Lusk was holding an umbrella in his left hand and a friend's hand in the other. Robert Randolph Jefferson, who claimed to be a nephew of the third president, "clandestinely" approached and violently attacked Lusk with a weapon. Lusk reached for his dirk knife, which fell to the ground. Bystanders separated the two men, as younger brother William H. Lusk Jr. arrived with a pistol. The crowd grabbed the latter's arm, and the weapon discharged into the crowd, landing in the thigh of a thirteen-year-old boy named Bradberry, who recovered.[139]

By 1856, when the railroad arrived, the *Jefferson Inquirer* had lasted long enough to be the third-oldest newspaper in Missouri, with only the *St. Louis Republican* and the *Palmyra Whig* being older. One of James Lusk's last decisions was to increase his publication to a daily. When he died at age forty, his younger brother took over.

Although William Lusk Jr. had apprenticed under his brother James, he had moved away from the paper's day-to-day operations. Among other things, he had joined John Knapp's Company C in the First Missouri Infantry serving in the Mexican-American War, including at the Battle of Matamoras.[140]

Like James before him, he was unexpectedly thrust into a demanding position. It was "a time of deep and exciting interest, at a crisis of great magnitude. It was a crisis of peril to those who had to act in it, but of subsequent glory to the actors. The invincibility of secession and disunion had become a proverbial expression and a war for the Union was only a question of time and full of terrific issues," Goodspeed's *1889 History of Cole County* said.[141]

William H. Lusk Jr. was the third in his family to operate the *Jefferson Inquirer*, prior to the Civil War. *Courtesy Wilson's Creek Battlefield.*

To make matters worse for the younger Lusk, the general assembly was reconsidering the costs of a public printer. One representative said in January 1861 that he was "not disposed to reduce the public printer's pay so that he could not make a living, but it appeared to be a pretty well-established fact that the public printer now got more than was necessary." (The late James Lusk had been paid more than $67,000 as public printer in 1856–57—that's more than $2 million in 2021. And Cheney and Corwin, public printers for 1858–59, were paid more than $123,000, equivalent to $3.9 million today.)[142]

In July 1859, William H. Lusk Jr. wrote his farewell in the *Jefferson Inquirer*: "Since the paper has been under our control, we have endeavored to pursue a straightforward, honorable course—doing what we conceived to be right, regardless of consequences.…We had not the feeling to proceed further in politics and shall seek other employment more congenial." He left it open for someone else to continue, but only if they continued their views: pro-Union, in favor of railroads, opposed to banks and anti-emancipation.[143]

Fearlessly patriotic for the Union and taking the same spirit he had poured into his press, young Lusk was correspondent to Frank Blair in St. Louis and then to Captain Nathaniel Lyon at the U.S. Arsenal, being present during the capture of Camp Jackson at the beginning of the Civil War.[144]

William Lusk Jr. enlisted in the U.S. Reserve Corps in June 1861 and in October was appointed assistant provost marshal. The following summer, he was commissioned a recruiting officer and raised four volunteer companies. In the fall of 1862, he was appointed captain of a company in the Tenth Missouri Cavalry and was soon promoted to major. His service included

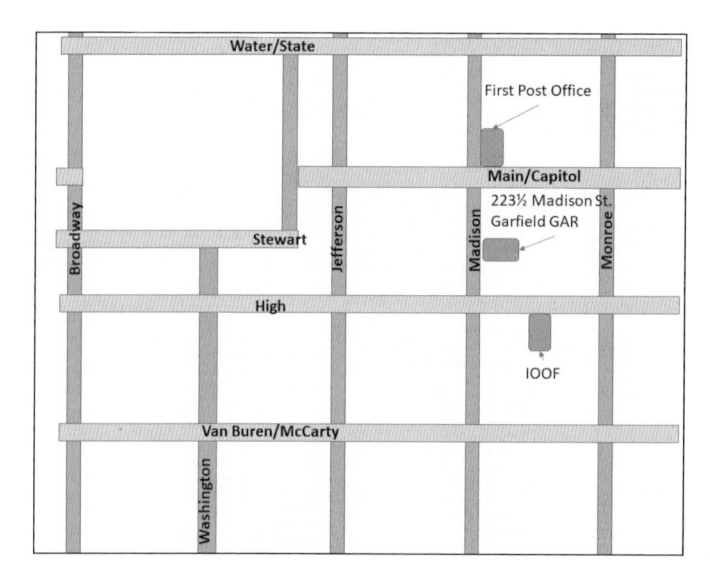

Map of locations associated with the Lusk family. Michelle Brooks.

taking part in the capture of Confederate officer and future governor John Marmaduke, three hundred prisoners and nine pieces of artillery at the Battle of Osage, Kansas, on October 25, 1864.[145]

After serving in his second war, Lusk returned to Jefferson City. He was chairman of the county Democratic committee for six years beginning in 1866, when he also ran for the legislature. That year, he also was elected as circuit clerk, to which he was reelected to serve thirty-two years.[146]

He was a commander of the James A. Garfield GAR Post no. 6 and continued to be fearless in his convictions, unswayed by public response.[147]

6

Three Corwins Make Newspapers, Radio

More than one media family crossed multiple generations, as well as modes of delivery, in Jefferson City. The Corwin family receives credit for the start of several print establishments, including the direct business ancestor of the *Jefferson City News Tribune*, and the first radio transmitter.

Charlton Jason Corwin established the *People's Tribune* in 1865, following the radical views of General Frank Blair, including support for the relocation of the state university from Columbia to Jefferson City. (Boone County was filled with southern-leaning residents, so the position was that the Capital City was a stronger postwar choice.)[148]

Within a year, Corwin sold control to his partner Joseph F. Regan. The *People's Tribune* was absorbed by the Tribune Printing Company in 1880 and merged with the *Cole County Democrat* in 1910. In 1927, the Edward Winter–Robert Goshorn partnership merged it with their *Daily Post* as the *Post Tribune*, which served the community for years as the Sunday newspaper.

New York–born C.J. Corwin began in Missouri newspapers about 1853, arriving in Jefferson City before 1856, when he married Sarah Frances Basye, the daughter of wealthy and influential businessman Alfred Basye. In 1857, he took over the *Metropolitan* newspaper, started in 1849 by Hampton L. Boone and John McCracken, and changed the name to the *Jefferson Examiner*. Two years later, Corwin sold that newspaper to W.G. Cheney, along with the public printing contract.[149]

After the Civil War, he opened and sold the *Tribune* before moving his family to Kansas City in 1867. There, C.J. Corwin was the principal editor of the *Kansas City Advocate* and soon the sole owner. He later joined the *Kansas City Evening News*, but his Democratic sentiments did not fit with its reorganization in May 1876. So, he returned to Jefferson City, working for the *Daily State Journal*. Then, Corwin joined C.J. Gundelfinger at the Jefferson City *Daily Eclipse* in 1880, where his son Charlton "Charly" Basye also worked as a newsboy.

Corwin moved to Sedalia in 1882, starting the *New Age* prohibition-supporting newspaper. By January 1883, he had bought out the thirty-year-old *Sedalia Eagle Times* and closed it. C.J. Corwin moved to Aspen, Colorado, in 1890 to work on the *Aspen Mail* with former *Sedalia Democrat* publisher Colonel John D. Russell.

C.J. Corwin started his last newspaper, the *Republican*, in 1900 in Jefferson City.

His son Charly Corwin advanced to printer's devil at the *Daily State Journal* and then reporter with the *Tribune*, which his father had started thirty years earlier. When that paper was sold to the *Cole County Democrat* at the end of 1909, Charly, like his father, started the independent, morning *Daily Capital News* on February 1, 1910.[150]

Charly Corwin and his sister Mary operated the Corwin News Agency, a bookstore, newspaper stand and musical instrument shop at 220 Madison Street and later behind his home on McCarty Street, from 1894 to 1936.[151]

Unlike C.J. Corwin's defeats in political campaigns (at least three), Charly Corwin was elected as Cole County's state representative in 1924.[152] C.J. and Charly both were active in the Democratic Party. The elder was a leader in the early statewide prohibition efforts, and the younger focused on local matters, including serving for decades on the library board.

In the backyard of Charly Corwin's 117 East McCarty Street home, his son Willis Porter Corwin taught himself how to set up a Marconi-style radio antenna, a wooden tower and a radio station in a shack in the backyard. From age thirteen, his interest in the phenomenon of wireless had him reading magazines and building his machine piece by piece. ("Wireless" means electro-state-eletromagnetic waves.) His call sign at 9ABD was appointed an official relay station of the American Radio Relay League in December 1915.[153]

The first message sent from his home station was on January 9, 1916, for local printer Hugh Stephens to his father, E.W. Stephens, in Columbia. That was followed the next month by participation in a national test, in which a

Hidden History of Jefferson City

Willis Porter Corwin taught himself as a young teenager how to build a wireless radio, as well as a tower in his backyard in the 100 block of East McCarty Street. *Courtesy Kent Trimble.*

Media

Colonel Nicholson at the U.S. Rock Island Arsenal sent a message in honor of President George Washington's birthday through wireless amateurs from Davenport, Iowa, to 37 governors and 137 mayors, including Governor Elliott W. Majors and Mayor Cecil Thomas.[154]

The Jefferson City Radio Club of the 1930s said Willis Corwin had a "key station on the cross-country relay trunk line."[155]

On the night of January 27, 1917, he received and re-transmitted three Morse code messages, part of the first one-way American, transcontinental message relay. Then, on February 15, 1917, his was one of five stations to be part of the first two-way relay of amateur radio stations from the East Coast to the West Coast and back in only eighty minutes, "an unheard of feat in those days," according to Mid-Mo Amateur Radio Club former president Kent Trimble.[156]

Willis Porter Corwin.
Courtesy Kent Trimble.

Only a few months later, the friendly amateur radio operators, who spoke nightly, made their last sign-offs. The government had asked that all stations be dismantled so that "no vagrant messages shall ply the air" in the era of looming war.[157]

After the U.S. government required him to remove his amateur antenna, Willis Corwin was the first man in Jefferson City to enlist in World War I. He graduated in May 1917 and then joined the U.S. Naval Reserve as a chief electrician (radio) in France, as well as a wireless operator aboard the troop ship en route to Europe, which had caught fire on its Atlantic crossing. Afterward, he also served as chief radio operator at naval installations in the Great Lakes area.[158]

Corwin returned from his military duty in November 1919. Wartime bans on radio use were being lifted, and several amateur enthusiasts sought his help to put up transmitters. The local Jefferson City Radio Club organized in 1920, and new HAMs were starting where Willis Corwin had been before the war.[159]

Willis Corwin attended the University of Missouri–Columbia, where in the fall of 1920 he helped fellow engineering student Nelson Nebel set up a student radio station at his home in Columbia. At the time, Willis Corwin held a first-grade commercial license from the U.S. Department of Commerce.[160]

The next year, Corwin experimented at the university with vacuum-tube transmission. This early experimentation gave him the expertise to help set up the state agriculture department's marketing bureau with a radio station. WOS was the first of its type west of the Mississippi River with a broadcasting license.

Corwin was the natural expert to turn to.

WOS was the first commercial AM broadcast station in the Capital City, the first state-owned station and among the first standard stations in the nation. D.C. Rogers, assistant marketing commissioner of the state and federal boards of agriculture, proposed the idea of a state-owned broadcast in 1921. It received immediate approval from department leaders but not state funding for a modern station and powerful transmitter.[161]

In August 1921, Corwin helped create a makeshift wireless system and aerial tower from the Capitol dome. An urgent matter arose at the state grain and warehouse commission in Jefferson City, while most officials were in Sedalia at the Missouri State Fair. The system allowed the question to be answered in short time.[162]

In February 1922, Rogers, Corwin and others made a homemade, low-power transmitter that reached a small area around the Capitol. With improvised equipment, the Capitol station sent out its first marketing news reports: daily livestock and grain prices.[163]

The general assembly released appropriations for a state marketing station late in the spring 1922 session. Missouri was the third contract for Western Electric for equipment and installation of a transmitter, but bureaucratic delays caused WOS to be the twelfth standard station erected in the nation in August 1922. Corwin was the first announcer and engineer.[164]

Since few farmers had radios in 1922, those who did were asked to write down the information and share it with fellow farmers in their area and with the local press. In 1927, a radio was deemed a farm business investment, and the number in Missouri jumped to sixty thousand.

Willis Corwin also superintended the construction of the *St. Louis Post-Dispatch*'s KSD radio station and stayed on as its first chief engineer, pioneering wire-photo transmission. Willis was part of the skilled radio and telephone men who were involved in refining the methodology used to transmit President Calvin Coolidge's address to Congress, the first time a president was heard over radio waves. As KSD's chief operator, he stayed in the station until 3:00 a.m. several days during the test period to listen to phonograph records being played and newspaper articles being read from

Media

Washington, D.C., and carried over telephone circuits to KSD and five other national stations.[165]

Sadly, Willis Corwin was declared insane, and his father was given custody of his affairs. At age thirty, he was admitted to the Veterans Home in Knoxville, Iowa, where he died twenty-nine years later. He is buried at the Jefferson City National Cemetery.

WOS continued for eleven years. Initially, content was limited to marketing news repeated several times each day. Three times each week, a cost-free entertainment program was arranged. That often turned out to be from inmates from the Missouri State Penitentiary. As time went on, programming expanded. For example, in 1924, WOS broadcast one of the nation's first college football games.[166]

A later engineer, J.M. Don Witten, made one of the most memorable contributions. One of the inmate musical groups, Virgil Coombs' Missouri State Prison Band, a twenty-eight-piece inmate jazz band, featured the piano playing of Harry Snodgrass. Listeners would organize parties in the homes of those with radio sets, timed around the airing of the "King of Ivories" concerts on alternating Monday nights beginning in late 1923.[167]

At age twenty-seven, Snodgrass was caught in the act of holding up a confectioner's shop in St. Louis in 1923 and sentenced to three years in the MSP. Along with his fellow inmate-musicians, Snodgrass was transported down Capitol Avenue from the prison to the Capitol for the broadcast.[168]

Because the transmitter reached as far as Hawaii, Alaska and Puerto Rico, Snodgrass soon became a radio sensation. In October 1924, he was voted the most popular radio entertainer in a nationwide radio magazine contest. Witten placed second for most popular radio announcer in the same contest. Early on, the band averaged two thousand pieces of mail after a performance.[169]

The studio's dimensions being only fourteen by seventeen feet, the band was limited to nineteen members during recording.

Governor Sam A. Baker commuted his sentence, and Snodgrass was released in January 1925. The night before, he performed in the House Chambers in front of an audience of hundreds. He had accumulated more than $3,500 in gifts from fans. And station manager Witten resigned at WOS to be Snodgrass' manager, securing him a recording deal with the Brunswick Balke Collender Company. Several recordings are held at the Missouri State Archive.[170]

Another favorite show on this earliest local radio station was the *Schnitzelbankers*.

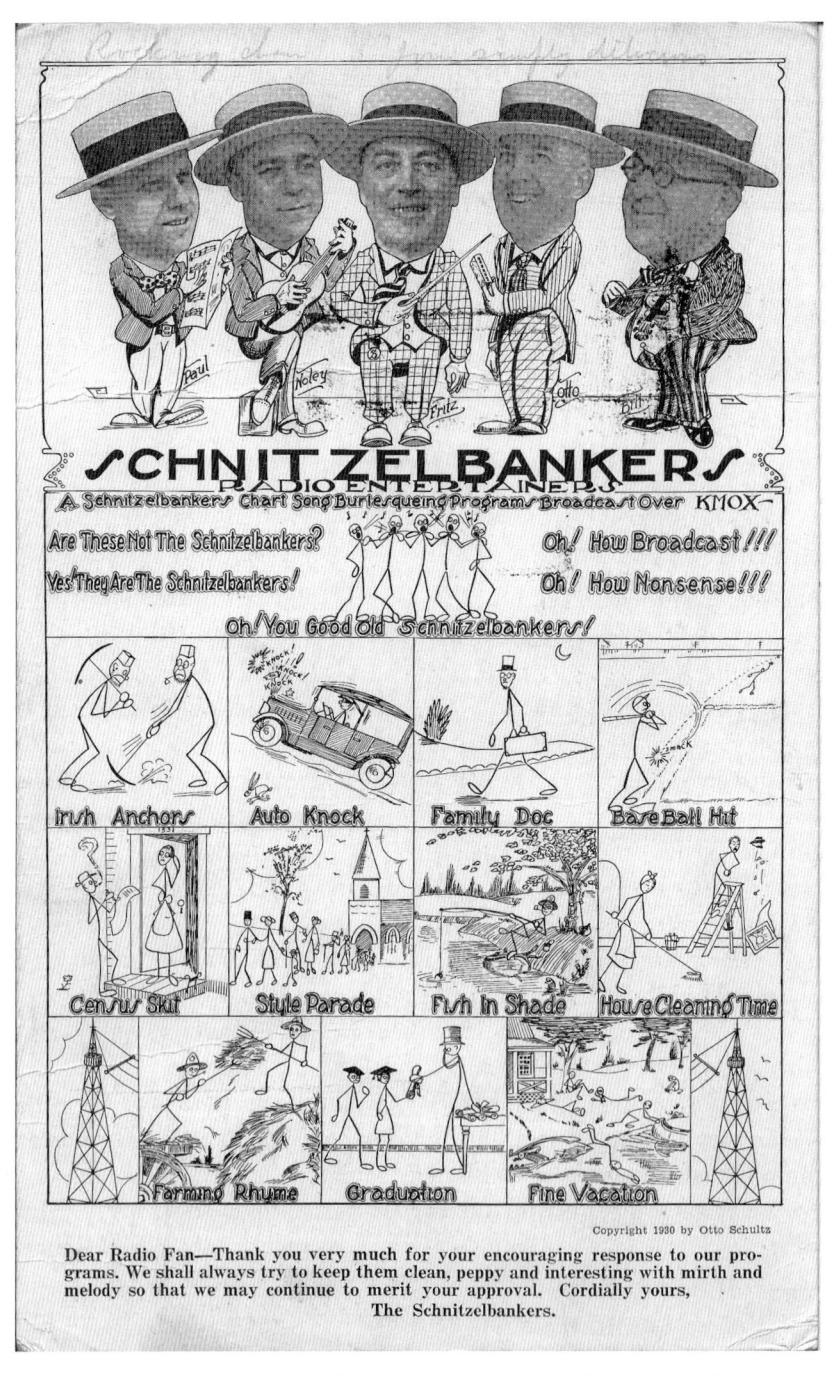

The *Schnitzelbankers* team performed on local and regional radio programs. *Courtesy the St. Louis Media History Foundation Archive.*

Media

Local immigrants' sons, Fritz Schott and Otto Schultz first put their comedic German-dialect characters and songs before the public on the Jefferson Theater stage in February 1914. Their skits were in demand for community events, particularly the annual Young Republican Association's Lincoln Day banquets across the state, though popularity dimmed during the World War I era.[171]

Other members came and went during a two-decade run: William Hoefer, Paul Radke, Nolan Wrightsman, Vic Lyons. Their shows on WOS from 1933 to 1935 followed three years of weekly shows on St. Louis' KMOX. Fan mail proved their routine's popularity, and repeat contracts and sponsors validated their talent. They were the pride of their hometown, receiving praise from all corners when they first received the St. Louis contract.[172]

The *Gasconade County Republican* described their entertainment as "always something new, unexpected, interesting, entertaining, thought-inspiring, well-charged with homespun philosophy, witty as well as naïve and presented in pleasing harmony and charm."[173]

But the men had families and businesses in Jefferson City that needed their attention. Schultz owned a shoe store uptown, and Schott was a clothier and real estate agent. Thankfully, their fans heard another two years on the local WOS station when the Schnitzelbankers left KMOX.

WOS was transferred to the Missouri Highway Patrol in July 1933. That institution's interest was in broadcasting wanted-men information. The station continued its entertainment programs until early 1936, when WOS ended and a low-wave police broadcast station, KIUK, replaced it.[174]

Radio listeners were not without a local station for long. *News Tribune* owner Robert C. Goshorn revived the WOS call letters in January 1937. The "K" was added by the communications commission. All stations west of the Mississippi River must start with the letter *K*. And so the station's motto became "Keep Watching Our State."[175]

Its location on the AM dial has moved. It sat at 1240 AM from 1941 to 1999, when it landed at its current home of 950. Goshorn also created Capital Broadcasting in the 1940s, launching the second FM station in the state, which ran from 1948 to 1958.[176]

The first KWOS offices were in the second floor of the Hough building at the corner of Adams and Capitol. The mansion had been built in 1884 by Fred Knaup, who made his wealth by owning the City Hotel. For many years, it was the residential showplace of the city before it was sold to the Houghs. Unfortunately, fire destroyed the state-of-the-art studio and building on December 4, 1940.[177]

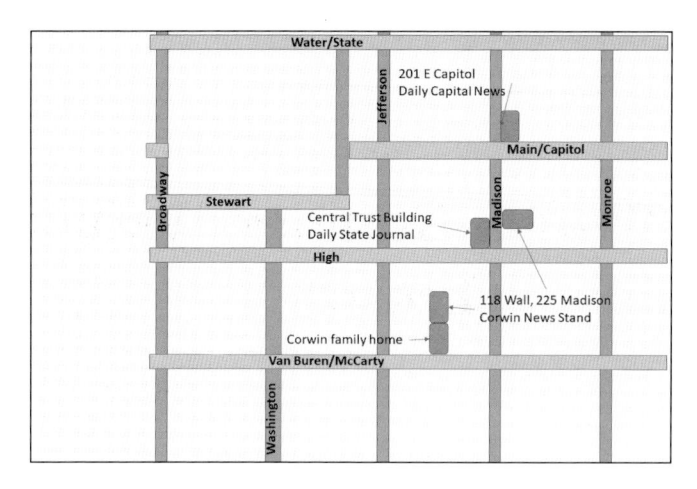

Map of locations associated with the Corwin family. *Michelle Brooks.*

Land on St. Mary's Boulevard at Beck Street, on the north side of US 50, directly opposite the White Way baseball park, was purchased from Bill Dulle to erect the 225-feet steel radio tower.[178]

Pemberton Gordon, who left WOS in 1935, was thrilled to return as the first manager of KWOS. He had lived in Jefferson City since 1908, served in the U.S. Marines during World War I and then graduated from the Rolla School of Mines in 1923. His first radio gig was in Texas, where he found that audiences liked his voice as much as he liked the work. Between his time with WOS and KWOS, he was a senior engineer in the Works Progress Administration.[179]

February 1, 1937, was the first commercial day with full programming, including a program by the Capitol Avenue Christian Church and the Johnny Muessig program. Muessig was a member of the Frankie & Johnny Band and then the Johnny Boys, playing across central Missouri. He hosted a morning show, worked in sales, served as a disc jockey and later was an owner during his more than thirty-five years with KWOS.

A beloved fixture in the community, Muessig joined the staff in 1951, broadcasting early farm and weather reports and later playing country-and-western music. He also was a U.S. Navy pilot and instructor at the Jefferson City Air Field.

KWOS was one of the original radio stations to carry St. Louis Cardinal games, from 1938 to 2006, and was considered a great step forward for the community at the time it went on the air. As with many ventures, it was initially a money loser and took years to build up business. Today, it is owned by Zimmer Radio Group.[180]

7
THE WINTER-GOSHORN-WELDON LEGACY

The year 1927 marked the turning point in Capital City journalism. The same man who would consolidate all print media under one roof also would put the first private radio station on the air and spark the vision of the area's first television station.

Robert C. Goshorn came from an Iowa newspaper family to partner with Warrenton newspaper publisher Edward H. Winter. Six years later, the latter had served as lieutenant governor and Goshorn had bought out his shares of a growing company. Winter had been in the midst of three terms as Warren County representative when they made the initial purchase of what would become the *Jefferson City News Tribune*.

Winter grew up on a Warren County farm. He was injured in a tornado as a teenager, making him unfit for farm life. He attended Central Wesleyan College in Warrenton and the University of Chicago before buying the *Warrenton Banner* in 1906. He was elected president of the Missouri Press Association in 1926, his last year with the *Banner*.[181]

Goshorn-Winter first bought the oldest newspaper in town, the *Jefferson City Tribune*, and soon after that purchased the twenty-four-year-old *Daily Post*, which was combined as the *Post Tribune* in 1933. The next step was to expand the operation and facility, installing a twenty-page rotary press. When the partners bought the twenty-two-year-old *Capital News* in 1932, they created a print monopoly that hadn't been seen in the Capital City since Calvin Gunn's more than a century earlier.[182]

The present *Jefferson City News Tribune* building at 210 Monroe Street opened in June 1932. *Michelle Brooks collection.*

Four years after Goshorn-Winter swept into the Capital City newspaper world, they erected the present building at 210 Monroe Street. That same year, the Phillips Pipeline installed its first tank, the state highway patrol was introduced, Kiwanis celebrated its tenth anniversary and Second Baptist Church was destroyed by fire.[183]

Architects Kennerly and Steigemeyer used brick and Bedford cut stone with terra-cotta trim for the impressive building, modern for its day. Originally, two symmetrical entrances faced Monroe Street leading to a large public lobby and the general office. The floors were of black-and-white terrazzo, and the lobby was accented with columns, pilasters and beamed ceilings.[184]

The *News Tribune* building's interior initially had two perimeter stairways leading up to a now-enclosed mezzanine that once featured bronze railings. Here, Winter and Goshorn each had his own office. The hallways then led to the advertising department on one side and the news department on the other. A library divided the Republican-leaning *Post Tribune* newsroom from that of the Democratic-leaning *Daily Capital News*.[185]

The third floor, today the business offices and display advertising, originally was rented to organizations including the Girl Scouts and the United Press Service. Notably, the floor was built of reinforced concrete, able to carry a load of four hundred pounds per square foot, compared to an average office load of forty pounds per square foot. (In theory, it could have held a press.)[186]

The basement housed the presses for seventy-five years, until the new plant on Schotthill Woods Road opened in 2006. The first press at 210 Monroe Street was hot-type, then was changed to linotype in the 1940s. Cold-set printing was introduced in the 1970s and remained until today's MAN Roland Uniset 75 press.

The ambitious Iowan brought a new dignity and professionalism to Capital City journalism. Among his first changes, Goshorn dropped page-one ads and added sports and cartoons.[187]

"Dad always thought of the good of the community, and my mother was very active in the community," Betty Weldon said.[188]

The son of the previous *Tribune* owner, Art Koester, continued to work in the composing room as foreman. "Bob Goshorn was an energetic man who wanted to improve the quality of the newspapers," Koester recalled. "He was a driving man who expected you to do your job and do it well."[189]

Goshorn's father had been the publisher of the Winterset, Iowa paper for half a century. After graduating from Iowa State University, Goshorn served as the business manager of the *Daily Inter Lake* in Montana. During the First World War, he was a commissioned officer serving stateside. Then, he was manager at his father's newspaper for four years before becoming publisher of the *Eagle Grove Times-Gazette* in 1921.

Part of the professionalism Goshorn brought to Jefferson City was more objectivity and less political myopia. He told his reporters, including future business manager Bob Blosser, to "get the news, to print the news. Don't be dissuaded. Don't be intimidated or bribed. The office is in back of you." Blosser said, "I like to think that we've kept some people on the straight and narrow."[190]

The editorial direction of the morning and evening papers, holding differing political views, were led by Lawrence Lutkewitte and Kelly Pool, both with close local ties. Blosser said they were "both devoted journalists, their differing philosophies gave the *Daily Capital News* and *Post Tribune* distinct editorial character."[191]

By 1936, less than a decade after arriving in the state, Goshorn was elected president of the Missouri Press Association. The next year, he opened radio station KWOS.[192]

When Goshorn died in 1953, his unfulfilled dream of opening a local television station was pursued by his only daughter, Betty. She used her father's initials as the call letters: KRCG. She was the first woman in the nation to launch a television station and operated it from sign-on in 1955 until it was sold to the Kansas City Southern Railroad Company in 1966.

In May 1954, the competition—the Durwood family, which owned the local movie theater—withdrew its interest in Channel 13, saying of Betty, "I know of no one better able to operate a successful television station in Jefferson City."[193]

When KRCG went on the air on February 13, 1955, it reached thirteen counties. Betty's son Gifford pulled the switch for the first day of operations, which amounted to six hours. The 105,000-watt station transmitted from a tower 1,400 feet above sea level. In May of that year, she attended the Republican National Convention, where President Dwight Eisenhower addressed the National Association of Radio and Television Broadcasters in Washington, D.C.[194]

At the end of 1955, she and her mother held a joint Christmas party for about 170 employees and their spouses from their three companies—newspaper, radio and television—at their Callaway Hills Farm. At the time, R.L. Rose was general manager of the newspaper, Blosser of the new KRCG and E.A. Richter at the radio station. What became the annual *News Tribune* Christmas party continued through the twenty-first century, though it changed into a service where employees helped provide gifts and a party for local children in need.

Goshorn's wife and Betty's mother, Lenore Rhyno, had helped with the newspaper operations while also being active in society. She was instrumental in the organization of Girl Scouts in Jefferson City and was a member of the first Jefferson City park board. "It was through her untiring efforts that the day camp and girl scout cabin on Green Berry road came into being in the 1930s," her 1959 obituary said. The Goshorn home at 1720 Hayselton Drive passed to Betty, as did ownership of all of the media holdings.[195]

The family moved to Jefferson City on Betty Goshorn's fifth birthday, first staying at the old Capitol Hotel. She grew up at 1220 Moreland Avenue and was involved in dance, children's theater and the First Presbyterian Church. Weldon attended the old Moreau Heights Elementary School, Mount Vernon Seminary in Washington, D.C., and then Mount Holyoke College in Massachusetts.[196]

Mrs. Weldon showed a marked interest in international awareness, as a child giving presentations on other countries at club meetings and as a young adult participating in the International Relations Club at Mount Holyoke. With her father, she participated in UNESCO (United Nations Educational, Scientific and Cultural Organization), serving as the Missouri executive secretary in 1949. That same year, she was appointed

Betty Weldon visits with Edward R. Murrow (*right*). *Courtesy* Jefferson City News Tribune.

social director as an alumni for Mount Holyoke's Institute on the United Nations, which included hosting First Lady Eleanor Roosevelt and Indian ambassador Vijaya Pandi.[197]

She was a combination of her father's news sense and business force, as well as her mother's disposition as hostess and community supporter. Her first job in the newspaper world was on the society page, her first column being about women's hats. Just after graduating from college in 1943, young Betty covered Harry Truman's nomination for president.[198]

Also during the war, her personal yacht at Lake of the Ozarks, the *Jetty Jinx*, was loaned to the federal government for coastal patrol service.[199] In the 1950s, she covered major stories, including the prison riot and a great flood, where she threw off the reporter's cap to help Jennie Allen rescue people.[200]

In 1973, Mrs. Weldon oversaw the press change from Linotype to early computerization and from letterpress to forty-page offset press. They didn't miss an edition in the changeover.[201]

Due to Federal Communications Commission regulations, the company had to let go of her father's work and her own in 1966, selling KWOS and KRCG.[202]

In 1987, the *News Tribune* had the largest circulation in central Missouri, reaching 38,500 households in ten counties. After Weldon's death in 2007, the *News Tribune* and Central Missouri Newspapers Inc. were purchased by the Arkansas-based WEHCO Media.[203]

As the head of the only media company in town, Weldon had held an influence that drew politicians and businessmen to seek out her favor. And she was benefactor to several organizations in town, often anonymously.

Weldon also invested heavily in the welfare of challenged children. She donated a building to educate handicapped children, known as the Goshorn Handicapped Center, which merged later with other schools to become today's Special Learning Center. The center opened in 1960 at 1719 St. Mary's Boulevard and included a home for the Cole County Cerebral Palsy Training Center, the Cerebral Palsy Clinic of Central Missouri and the adult workshop, doctor's offices and therapy rooms.[204]

She made sure the children of prisoners at the Cole County Jail had gifts at Christmas, and she hosted an annual holiday party for hundreds of underprivileged children. She was responsible for the first cancer fundraising drive in Missouri and was a member of the Missouri State Cancer Board. The local Zonta Club's lifetime achievement award is named in her honor.

Like her father, she made community leadership a priority. In 1950, at age twenty-eight, she was elected vice-chairman alongside Chairman Joe DeLong of the reactivated Greater Jefferson City Committee, formed under mayor and longtime newspaperman Lawrence Lutkewitte.[205] She was involved with clubs like the Olive Ewing Dallmeyer Music Club, the Cole County Historical Society and the American Red Cross.

Also an animal lover, Weldon raised champion American saddlebred horses and established Callaway Hills, a major shelter for animals without homes. Her attachment to these four-legged mammals may have started when she was seven and her two-year-old Boston terrier, Bozo, strayed in April 1929. Weldon ran reward ads for more than four months.[206]

She won the American Royal at age twenty with her beloved Kate Shriver and was a force in the saddlebred horse world for decades.[207] She continued winning in 1946 with her three-gaited Fourth Estate. President Ronald Reagan and actor William Shatner visited the stables on more than one occasion.

At one time, Callaway Hills was the largest privately owned American saddlebred breeding operation in the world and the home of many champions, the best-known being Will Shriver, named for her great-grandfather, a Union cavalry man. It won the five-gaited World Grand Championship in 1976.

Media

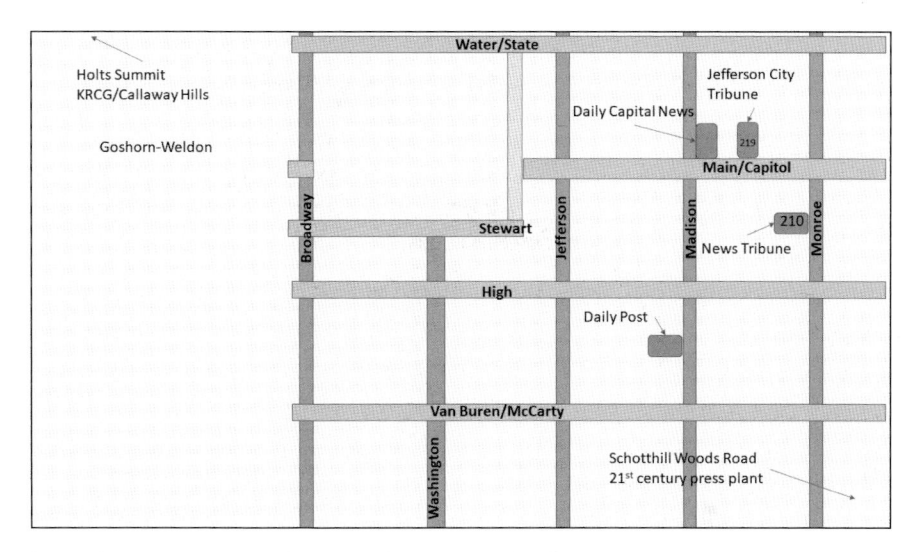

Map of locations associated with the Goshorn-Weldon family. *Michelle Brooks*.

She was chairman of the Missouri Horse Racing Commission in the 1980s and 1990s. And Mrs. Weldon initiated the creation of a U.S. Postal Service stamp series honoring four well-known horse breeds, including the American saddlebred.

Mrs. Weldon and Will Shriver were inducted into the St. Louis National Charity Horse Show Hall of Fame, and Will Shriver was named Horse of the Century as part of the American Royal's centennial celebration. His image was used in 1999 by the Breyer Horse Company for its collector's model. Mrs. Weldon received the first-ever Medal for Distinguished Service to the American Saddlebred Horse from the American Royal in 2000.

Part III
MOVING FORWARD

SELECTED FOR ITS PROXIMITY to the Missouri and Osage Rivers, the main frontier arteries at the time, Jefferson City has had to keep up with changing transportation modes.

Native Americans and trappers, mostly Frenchmen, had drifted by canoe or mackinaw down these rivers or walked the narrow trails through the ancient forests. That would not serve the seat of government.

Able men like Burr H. McCarty brought their knowledge of horses to provide livery and stagecoach services.

And the ferry business was a necessity for contact with the north side of the river, except during the winter months, when the unaltered Missouri River was wide and shallow and could be crossed by foot and wagon. Many eager entrepreneurs, like Captain Jefferson T. Rogers, took the challenge to provide first horse-powered and later steam-powered ferry services back and forth.

The railroad arrived in 1856, bringing more passengers and more growth to the city. Men like the Grimshaws became stalwarts for the community, working for the railroad and serving the city's future.

While personal automobiles entered the scene at the turn of the twentieth century, the potential of air travel captured the imagination of community leaders. The second Jefferson City Air Field lasted less than two decades but made history nonetheless.

The Capital City required access, and it was up to entrepreneurs and men with know-how to take the risk to make it happen.

8
Crossing the River

Of the many resourceful and entrepreneurial early settlers, ferryboat captain Jefferson T. Rogers was one of the most interesting. In the early 1800s, the common water modes were canoes, keelboats, mackinaws or French bateaux. The first steamboat would not be seen this far west until the *Independence* stopped for the night in 1819 at the village of Marion.[208]

As a teenager, Rogers first traveled the Missouri River from St. Louis west with his family to Boonville. Later, they returned east to settle in Callaway County. The Rogers family lived off the land and provided ferry service to the north side of the Missouri River. Like many early pioneers, Rogers and his family ate bear meat, venison, turkey, fish, wild honey and vegetables they hunted or gathered themselves. They began as tanners and tried milling for a while, but then turned to ferrying.[209]

The established French settlement of Cote Sans Dessein was the only real population center in mid-Missouri during pre-statehood. As a young man, Rogers attended King balls, wearing moccasins and a hunting shirt, to mingle with other nearby families. He later was among several local men caught gambling at faro in December 1826, including Josiah Ramsey Jr., Alexander Gordon and Hardin Casey.[210]

Arriving when only a few log cabins had been set up before him, Jefferson Rogers left the north side of the river to make his own home in the wilderness-turned–mud street Capital City. He was friends with area Native Americans. When Rogers asked them about the origins of the now-removed burial mounds on Capitol Hill and College Hill, among other river bluff sites, the indigenous people said the mounds had been here long before the Osage and Missouri Nations.[211]

By age twenty-five, Rogers had received a ferry license from the Callaway County court. He and his father, Thomas, worked a horse-powered ferry, carrying both freight and passengers to Jefferson City, until his father died in 1835. The sought-after ferry license passed between Rogers and a handful of boat operators in the next few decades.[212]

In 1839, Rogers partnered with other early rivermen like E.B. Cordell and John Yount to operate the first steam ferry in Jefferson City.[213] Yount held the land for the Callaway County side landing, and Rogers married Yount's daughter Kizzia. Although the landing at the north end of Jefferson Street was the most prominent, it was not the only landing at the Capital City. Boats also could offload at Chestnut Street near the Missouri State Penitentiary, and Rogers' Landing was at Harrison Street.

If the uptown area was the first neighborhood of the new Capital City, the Goose Bottoms, later known as the Millbottom, was its second. Rogers bought up dozens of lots in this area at the foot of Richmond Hill, east of Bolivar Street.[214]

Rogers' homestead took up much of the 600 block of Water Street, today state parking and a Union Pacific yard. In front of his large stone home was his ferry landing on Harrison Street. Built in 1840, the Rogers mansion's elegance was said to be second only to the Thomas Lawson Price mansion at the southwest corner of High and Washington Streets. Rogers lived there until his death in 1880.[215]

At the turn of the twentieth century, the home was razed to make room for facilities for the Missouri Pacific branch to Boonville. But the stone was reused in the Carnegie library, now county offices, on Adams Street.[216]

In 1848, Rogers installed a new steam ferry, which could cross to the Callaway County shore in less than three minutes. His operation at the Harrison Street landing included "good and substantial floats, landing boats, horses and wagons." The Missouri River crossing at Jefferson City became a major operation; travelers headed south from Hannibal and other points north could save up to fifty miles.[217]

Before the U.S. Corps of Engineers dredged the Missouri River into a deep and narrow flow, it was many times wider and fairly shallow. The colder winters of the nineteenth century froze the muddy waves, preventing ferry crossings. That's when travelers and capitalists turned to horse-drawn carriages, like the one driven by Charles Glenn over the ice-covered river.[218]

Moving Forward

The home of Jefferson T. Rogers at Rogers Landing near Harrison Street and the Missouri River's edge rivaled the Thomas Lawson Price home in its beauty. *Courtesy Cole County Historical Society.*

Charles Fountain Glenn was seventeen when he enlisted in the Confederate army's Wood Battalion Cavalry in 1864 at Boonville. He was paroled at Shreveport the following year. In 1877, he became a well-befriended janitor at the Missouri Supreme Court building, working there for forty years. He was known for his ingenuity, such as laying gravel walks for the court building.[219]

Rogers was more of a frontiersman than an urban dandy. One account said he was "almost as broad as he was long" and "could not fail to attract notice as he passed." He was a man of tender dignity and would brawl over any slight. He happened to be "a scrapper of unusual ability."[220]

Once a man came to town with the intention to fight Rogers, meeting him on Main Street just west of Weir's Creek. As Rogers undressed for the fight, he revealed a "torso covered in a mass of black hair." The stranger reportedly said he did not want to "fight no damn bear" and proposed they "liquor up instead."[221]

Although gruff in appearance, Rogers was a generous man, sometimes to a fault. His grandson Arthur Rogers recalled that the ferryman "helped many poor fellows in distress…turned no man hungry from his door, nor closed his ears to the appeals of charity."[222]

Like many of Jefferson City's early leaders with southern roots, he was for the Union but also for the continued legal use of slavery. Just prior to the war, he had represented Cole County at the statewide Pro-Slavery Convention in Brunswick. During the Civil War, Rogers put up security at least three times for local men who had been charged with aiding the enemy.[223]

He was interested not only in developing his family's fortune, but also in the success of this infant city. He saw river transportation as an opportunity. He also did not fear competition, introducing the resolution in 1841 to the city council authorizing fellow ferry operator James A. Crump to set up across Weir's Creek, only blocks east of Rogers Landing.[224]

After the city incorporated in 1839, Rogers served on the city council in 1840 and was elected the fourth mayor in 1844, serving his first term in between terms by pioneer newspaperman Calvin Gunn. In all, he served ten times as mayor and several times as president of the city council during his six terms as a councilman.[225]

One issue he fought for in those early years of municipal government was attendance for a council quorum, suggesting a two dollars fine for absenteeism. It did not pass. And in the sparse winter of 1856, he offered to keep the city's horses and mules in his feed barn free of charge until the spring rather than seeing them sold.[226]

At the state level, he was appointed paymaster general under governors Robert Stewart (1857–61) and Claiborne Jackson (1861–62 in exile).

Rogers shifted his attention from government to the county fair. In the fall of 1866, he was president of the Cole County Agricultural Association. He was pushing for repair and beautification of the buildings and grounds, which had been abused for years as a Union army campground, today part of McClung Park. He also saw that new drives and walks were leveled and graveled.[227]

Well aware of the power of the railroad, Rogers did not fight the new transportation mode but rather worked with it. In 1871, he was on the inaugural board of directors of the Jefferson City, Lebanon and Southwestern Railway, alongside Judge Arnold Krekel, Gerhard Dulle,

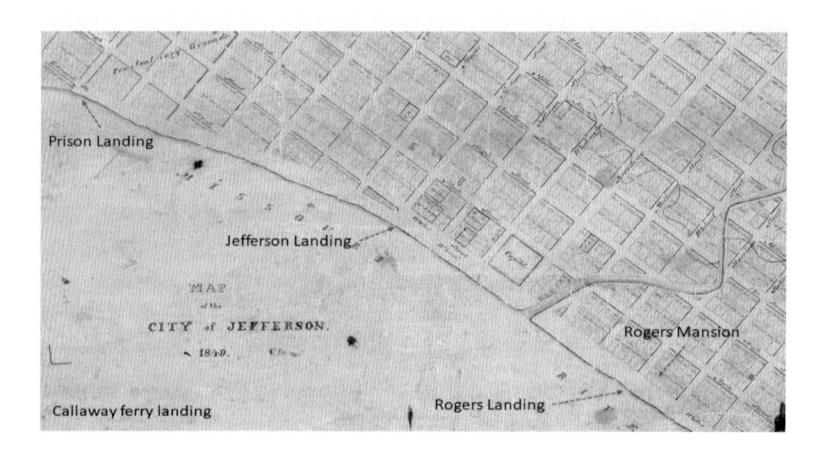

Jefferson T. Rogers map. *Courtesy Missouri State Archive. Paint by Michelle Brooks.*

H. Clay Ewing and other community leaders. When the deal to secure a Missouri Pacific roundhouse went through, Rogers sold much of his property in the Millbottom and influenced his neighbors to do the same.[228]

Rogers also was involved in building some of early Jefferson City with a steam sawmill he operated for a time on Water Street near Monroe. According to Dr. Robert Young's recollections, logs flowed down the Missouri River and were drawn by a tramway out of the river up to the mill. Until the railroad arrived, Rogers' mill and his warehouse did a thriving business and later provided railroad ties.[229]

Early twentieth-century local historian Lawrence Luetkewitte called Rogers a "Progressive, constantly espousing measures calculated to make the community a better place in which to live."[230] And twenty-first-century local historian Gary Kremer called him "one of the more intriguing figures whose life was intertwined with the development of the Millbottom."[231]

9
MAIL AND HOSPITALITY

Before the romantic attempts by John Butterfield and the Pony Express to cross the frontier, pioneer entrepreneurs like Thomas Lawson Price and Burr Harrison McCarty were carving the wilderness into a useful route for the centuries of transportation that has followed.

The National Road, or Cumberland Road, was on its way to reach Jefferson City when the seat of government arrived in 1826. One of the earliest stagecoach lines in Missouri began in 1819 from St. Louis to Franklin, north of the Missouri River. Like the city itself, roads had to be built from the state's growing population centers to the seat of government.[232]

The concept of the National Road, or the Cumberland Road, developed after the Revolutionary War to connect the spread-out nation and was authorized by President Thomas Jefferson in 1806. The U.S. mail routes crossed west of the Mississippi River into Missouri Territory in 1803, following from Louisville, Kentucky, to Vincennes, Indiana, to Cahokia, Illinois.[233]

In 1820, just before Missouri became a state, the National Road was funded to the Mississippi River and President James Monroe extended the postal routes farther into Missouri north of the river, from St. Charles through Cote Sans Dessein in Callaway County, to Franklin and all the way to Fort Osage.

Jefferson City was named the western terminus for the National Road in 1825, but funding dropped in the next decade, and the grand idea stopped at Vandalia, Illinois.[234]

Moving Forward

So it was up to entrepreneurs and their stagecoach routes to create the first roads connecting cities in the westernmost state in the union. As the roads grew in use, the stage routes might be dotted with relay stations, which might offer a barn, fresh horses, a nearby spring and a post office. Stagecoaches averaged about 5 miles per hour, not including stops to change drivers and horses, and an average day's trip might be 120 miles.[235]

Jefferson City's richest man, Price received the U.S. mail contract for St. Louis to Jefferson City in 1838. Before that, the early settlers had to depend on travelers' good nature to carry individual letters and parcels to destinations west.[236]

Thomas Lawson Price. *Courtesy Cole County Historical Society.*

The 139-mile land route went from St. Louis to St. Charles to Warrenton, then through Lewiston, Danville and Fulton. From Fulton, the stagecoach had to cross the Missouri River at Hibernia to reach Jefferson City.[237]

With the mail contract from Postmaster General Cave Johnson, Price started the first of several stage lines from the Capital City.[238] By 1840, lines also had been established south to Springfield and west to Independence, with offices at Young's City Hotel at the northwest corner of High at Madison Streets. And another eastern stage line worked out of Newman's National Hotel, also on High Street.[239]

In 1848, the stage route from St. Louis to Independence also stopped in Jefferson City, between Mount Sterling and Marion. The southern stage route left from Jefferson City for Van Buren, Arkansas, stopping at Moreau, Versailles, Warsaw, Salem, Bolivar, Springfield, McDonald and Cassville, then heading into Arkansas.[240]

A second eastern route was direct from Capital City to Capital City, first crossing the river north to Hibernia, then stopping in New Bloomfield, Fulton, Centreville, Shamrock, Middletown, Ashley, Bowling Green and Louisiana; then it went east across the Mississippi River to Springfield, Illinois.[241]

By 1850, a second route from St. Louis to Jefferson City had been added: Manchester to Union to Mount Sterling, then to Lisle and then Jefferson City. And to the west, the route to Warsaw was through Versailles and Cole Camp or to Independence by way of Marion, Boonville, La Mine, Arrow Rock, Marshall, Lexington, Wellington and Fort Osage.[242]

When Jefferson City incorporated in 1839, Price was elected its first mayor, serving two terms. At the same time, he built the Virginia Hotel at the northwest corner of High and Jefferson Streets. Then, in 1842, he built what was unanimously considered the most magnificent home in the Capital City, at the southwest corner of High and Washington.[243]

Price arrived at age twenty-two with significant wealth, left by his father's estate in Pittsylvania County, Virginia, and managed to increase it through his stage lines, manufacturing, mercantile and real estate. He was involved in the formation of the Capital City Bank, was an advocate for the railroads and served as president of the Jefferson Land Company.[244]

Relatives of his wife, Lydia Bolton, already lived in Jefferson City, inviting the young couple in 1832. Before his death in 1870, Price had served as lieutenant governor, state representative and congressman. Despite being an active Democrat and holding perhaps the highest number of enslaved people in central Missouri, Price was a loyal Unionist during the Civil War and often served as community diplomat.

Price's business partner in the stagecoach venture was fellow Virginian and livery owner Burr McCarty. When McCarty arrived in 1836, horseback or wagon was the only means to Jefferson City, other than the river. McCarty established the first livery, feed and sale stable—large enough for seventy-five animals—in Jefferson City after buying the entire block between Miller and McCarty, south of what was originally named Van Buren Street, following the pattern using presidential names. It was renamed by the general assembly in 1857 to McCarty Street. McCarty remained in the livery business for forty-five years, and many of his horses won premiums at the county fair.[245]

McCarty was reared and educated on a plantation in Loudon County, Virginia. Before arriving in Boonville in 1832, he studied at Virginia University in Charlotte and then worked horses through Kentucky, Alabama and Mississippi.[246] An 1885 newspaper article described Burr McCarty as having a "spirit of enterprise and energy…and warm hospitality."[247]

His wife, Alzira Hughes, had arrived in Jefferson City the day of the first Capitol fire, November 15, 1837, accompanying her sister and brother-in-law, Patsy and John Curry, who became proprietor of Price's Virginia Hotel.[248]

A natural host and storyteller, according to his grandson Wilbur, McCarty visited with his early passengers, mostly lawyers and politicians. At first, he invited some of these gentlemen to his modest frame home at 120 West Van Buren Street. He saw a need for these travelers' comfort upon their arrival.[249]

So, in June 1838, the McCartys made the first of several additions to their home and hotel, which maintained a seventy-year reputation for southern

Moving Forward

The Price mansion stood at the southwest corner of Washington and High Streets, where the Missouri Supreme Court is today. *Courtesy Missouri State Archive Summers Collection.*

hospitality and old-fashioned meals. This first expansion was aided by the same men working on the second state Capitol. A large addition, with a plantation-style veranda, considerably expanded the hotel in 1855.[250] *New York Tribune* reporter Junius Henri Browne described the McCarty House in 1861 as "an ancient hotel, a rambling structure built on several levels around a courtyard with wide galleries in the rear."[251]

The rooms held downy feather beds, and every part of the twenty-room building was pristine. Only the lighting changed in the hotel's interior during its decades of service, passing from candlelight to oil to gas in 1897.[252]

A mainstay was the front office's mantle and fireplace. "In the office there is still the old-time inn suggestion of warmth and good cheer, a fireplace in which the dry wood crackles and sends its embers up the chimney and its light out in the darkened room," Harry Norman wrote in the *St. Louis Republic*.[253]

At this source of light and heat, many politicians plotted their campaigns and the state's future. Frequent guests included Senator Thomas Hart Benton and Governors John Phelps, Sterling Price and B. Gratz Brown.[254]

One story McCarty was known to retell from the hotel's early years discussed when counties sent their sheriffs and collectors to settle accounts with the state treasurer. Their horses often were weighed down by the gold and silver they carried. And yet, robbery was little threat, and few houses, much less the hotel's doors, had locks.[255]

U.S. district judge John Phillips credited the McCarty House with "unbounded hospitality, home like simplicity and unsurpassed table." He delivered the eulogy for second-generation owner Ella McCarty. Of the hotel's founder, he recalled a man "bright with wit and stinging with sarcasm in the midst of interchange of repartee and discussion of leading men."

During the Civil War, Burr McCarty was found disloyal and a rebel sympathizer by the provost marshal. Early in 1861, the McCarty House was filled by as many as twenty newspaper correspondents—later dubbed the Bohemian Brigade—prior to General John Frémont's army arriving by steamer in September 1861.

McCarty refused to fly the Stars and Stripes at his hotel. And when a Union general requested to be quartered there, McCarty defiantly said he was full. The general angrily ordered a room to be freed up for him. Afterward, the general still did not care for the "air too full of secession" and ordered the entire house emptied. For a time, it served as barracks.[256]

When Confederate general Sterling Price made his doomed raid into Missouri from the south in 1864, Union troops again moved out the family and guests of the McCarty House. Holes were knocked through the brick walls for cannon and rifle fire, and the entire block with hotel and livery was barricaded. When the city was spared a full battle, the McCarty House served as one of the hospitals to care for those wounded in the skirmish.[257]

Perhaps the most sensational guest to stay at the McCarty House was outlaw Frank James on the night before his surrender to Governor Thomas Crittenden. This historic arrangement was made possible by newspaperman Major John N. Edwards, author of *Shelby and His Men* and *Shelby's Expedition to Mexico*. He was both a good friend with the McCartys and had served in the war with James and his notorious younger brother Jesse. Edwards served as middle man to make arrangements for James, who was living on the East Coast, to turn himself in following the assassination of his brother and fellow outlaw.

Moving Forward

Frank James checked into the McCarty House using an alias one evening in October 1882.[258] The next day, he walked the town unrecognized and stopped into the Capitol to arrange for his surrender, saying he was repentant and reformed. The following day, James stood before the governor, unstrapped his .44-caliber Remington revolver and said, "I want to hand over to you that which no living man except myself has been permitted to touch since 1861, and to say that I am your prisoner."[259]

James was then held in a room at the Basye Hotel, formerly the Rising Sun, operated by another southern-born hotelier, Susan Basye. That evening, nearly five hundred residents paraded through the city's oldest inn to view the famous criminal seated in his hotel room. Even Crittenden and his wife stopped in during their evening stroll.[260]

Seven years after negotiating this historic surrender, Edwards died in his bed at the McCarty House. Just months before, he had written a nice story about the hotel, praising its tradition and cookery. His death "created a profound sensation throughout the city," a newspaper reported. While awaiting the train to remove his remains to Dover, a "constant stream of sad and sorrowing friends passed in and out of the corridor." A funeral procession led by Governor David Francis (1889–93) followed from the hotel to the train station, with McCarty's daughter Ella traveling with her close friend, the widow Edwards.[261]

Ella McCarty took over the family business after her parents died in the early 1890s. She had attended Jefferson Female College. Classmates included Maria and Mary Jefferson, Cornelia Wells and Nannie Minor. She was a member of "society," attending balls in fanciful gowns and having her name listed in newspaper accounts of the most elite parties in the city. But she was equally impressive as a hotelier.[262]

Like her father, Ella did not fly the American flag over the McCarty House until 1898, after the battleship *Maine* exploded in a Cuban harbor, causing Congress to declare war and call five thousand soldiers from Missouri into the Spanish-American War. Former Union officer and frontier soldier Nelson Cole, who became a brigadier general in the U.S. Army, was a good friend of the McCarty family. Ella made a personal appeal to Governor Lon Stephens to make Cole's appointment to the state militia.[263]

Governor Stephens called Ella McCarty personally the day he did. In gratitude, she personally visited the governor, the general and several Jefferson City friends to inform them she would raise the Stars and Stripes above the old hotel.[264]

"This news was enough to shake the Capitol to its very foundation stone, and the flag-raising was one of the events of that year," the *St. Louis Republican* reported. The flag was waiving as General Cole and the volunteers marched to the train station.[265]

The cornerstone of McCarty hospitality was its genuine menu. Huge cuts of beef were roasted and chicken was fried. The coffee was perfection, and white biscuits and cornbread were served. Three women, enslaved by McCarty and Alzira, remained with the McCarty House after emancipation. It was their skill that built and sustained this reputation for a table of tasty plates.[266]

The traditions of the Virginia kitchen were brought by Cassandra Crump, who worked in the McCarty House kitchen for thirty-nine years from its opening. She reigned, and her assistants knew better than to offer suggestions, much less dispute her decisions. Never to be called "Cassie McCarty," Crump "put plenty of whisky in the mincemeat and an abundance of rum in the punch," the *Kansas City Star* reported.[267]

Among those in Crump's kitchen was Callaway County–born Mary Stokes, who began working in the hotel kitchen at age seven. In 1868, Stokes became Crump's assistant and in 1876 took over as the second and only other head cook for the hotel in its seventy-year history.[268]

Stokes continued with diligent attention to the old-fashioned recipes, including breakfast biscuits and cornbread for dinner. She was unwilling to leave her kitchen to anyone else, even when offered retirement with full pay, until the inn was converted to apartments in 1906.[269]

During the 1904 Democratic National Cnvention, held in Jefferson City, four newspapermen sent for meals from the McCarty House kitchen. Surprised at their meal, they later visited the hotel, and each gave Stokes a silver dollar as a tip of appreciation for her skill in the kitchen.[270]

Stokes, who went by "Aunt Mary," was joined around 1880 by head waiter Mary Jackson, who went by "Jack." After emancipation, the pair continued living in the former slave cabin behind the hotel, where they reared their children.[271]

Stokes' son Robert Wyatt Stokes no doubt received good training in hotel management while growing up in the McCarty House. He became the owner/operator, with his wife, Emily, of the New Moon Hotel at 209 Monroe Street, today a parking lot between First United Methodist Church and the Cole County Courthouse.[272]

Jack's children, Joshua, Bob and Sallie, worked and played at the hotel and were as well-known as she was among the prominent guests. The

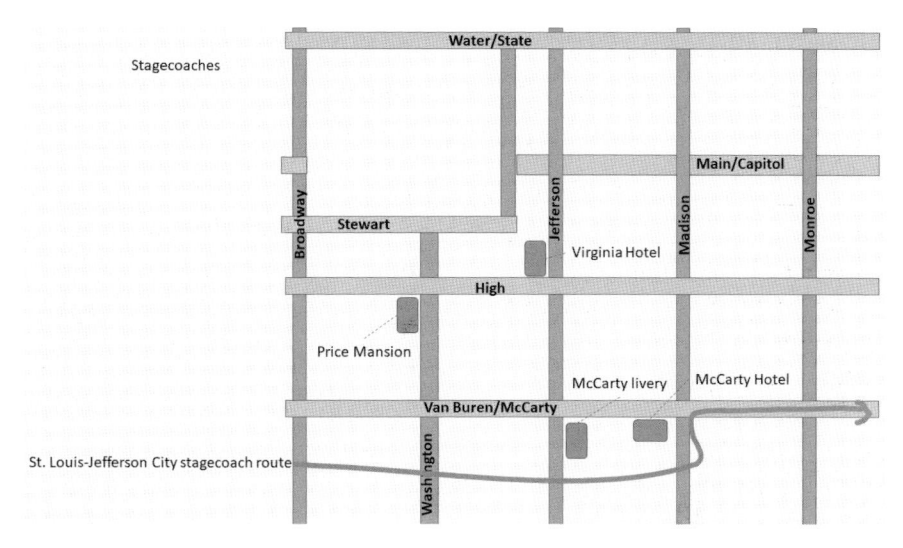

Map of early locations associated with stagecoaches. *Michelle Brooks*.

children were often found playing the card game grabouche, taught to them by Missouri Supreme Court judge William Marshall, in the home's sitting room, when they were not running errands or tending fires.[273]

"Every judge of the Missouri Supreme Court and every governor the state has had since Silas Woodson was the executive has been proud to claim an acquaintance with Jack," the February 10, 1901 *Kansas City Star* reported.[274]

Not only were these former slaves, now free women, held in high regard by all who knew them, but the McCarty family also compensated them well. When Stokes died in 1914, she owned her home on McCarty Street between Adams and Jackson, considerable shares in the Missouri Central Building and Loan Association and enough left over to provide an endowment for charity.[275]

10

RIDING THE RAILS

While the welcoming ambience of the Romanesque-revival Missouri Pacific Railroad depot delivered the romantic experience, Arthur Grimshaw and his father, Jonathan, provided travelers with their tickets and instructions through many of the city's critical decades.

The iconic red-brick station at the north end of Monroe Street was built in 1898.[276] The Missouri River Bridge had been built by city leaders two years earlier, allowing passengers to transfer to and from the Missouri, Kansas, Texas Railroad and the Chicago and Alton Railroad lines on the north side of the river. The city was growing, and with it, its transportation needs.

Local builder Henry Wallau followed the designs of E. Fischer, Missouri Pacific's bridge and buildings engineer. Mastering the carpentry trade in his home of Alsbach, Germany, Wallau arrived in Jefferson City in 1882. His first work was helping prominent local architect Fred Binder erect the present St. Peter Church. His first general contract was the Bockrath Shoe Store at 703 West Main Street in 1886.[277]

Wallau opened the Capital City Planing Company in 1891, with his workshop located on West Water Street, west of the Lohman Building, about where the state parking garage is today.[278] Many of his other century-old buildings remain in the city, including St. Peter School (1889), Nieghorn House Hotel (1892), St. Peter Hall (Sellinger Center), the Carnegie library (1901), Grace Episcopal Church (1898), the Cole County Courthouse (1896) and the Jacob Moerschel home on Swifts Highway (1907). Wallau also built

Moving Forward

The Missouri Pacific Railroad Station is an impressive brick building at the north end of Monroe Street. *Courtesy Missouri State Archives Bob Priddy Collection.*

the Capitol Brewery and ice plant, the G.H. Dulle Mill and St. Mary's Hospital, as well as other regional public buildings and Catholic churches.

During his seven terms as city alderman and two as mayor, Wallau saw several city improvements through to completion, including the roadways over Weir's Creek at Miller Street. He also led the St. Peter Benevolent Society for twenty years.[279]

In 1905, he partnered with the Kay Brothers to form the Jefferson City Sand Company, retiring from construction in 1912 to manage the sand business, located on the south side of the Missouri River in the Millbottom. The work was done by hand on a steep bank before steam and then electric machines became available. After his death in 1927, Wallau's sons, Al and George, took over the sand business and built the ninety-by-twenty-foot *J.H. Wallau* steamer, which pushed their barges for seventeen years.[280]

Wallau's impressive brick railroad station was a beneficial statement of permanence for a city working to overcome statewide doubts of its worthiness to retain the status of a capital city. At the time, the city's population was about ten thousand and expected to grow. The sizeable improvement from the modest location at the end of Adams Street reflected the railroad's shared optimism of growth.

The station had Carthage stone accents, similar to the Capitol building, and a roof of copper and slate. Inside, the floors were maple, the chandeliers

The Jefferson City Sand Company opened on the south side of the Missouri River. *Courtesy Cole County Historical Society.*

were oxidized copper and six-feet-high oak wainscoting covered the walls. The general waiting room was accented by a Roman brick mantel piece, but there also was a ladies' parlor and a gentlemen's smoking room. The building also housed the ticket office, telegraph office, a business hall and other office space, as well as an open second floor.[281]

As a seven-year-old, Bee Kiely Witcher recalled arriving "at the Missouri Pacific Railroad station heated by a big, pot-bellied stove. The gaslights cast flickering shadows all around the waiting room, while outside horse-drawn carriages waited to take travelers to their destinations."[282]

Arthur Grimshaw was in his third year as mayor when he took over the ticket agent duties for both Pacific and US Express after his father, Jonathan, retired in 1893. Where the father served only one term as city mayor, the son held the position six times. That year, Arthur Grimshaw also was elected the first chairman of the newly organized Commercial Club, forerunner of the Jefferson City Area Chamber of Commerce.[283]

The Grimshaw family's connection to railroads began early in England and spanned three generations.

Jonathan Grimshaw was born to a steady, industrious Baptist family in 1818, reared in an atmosphere of decency, honesty and comfort. He was apprenticed to a shoemaker, but it did not agree with his health. He used his leisure time to improve his writing and arithmetic skills. So, when his master left the shoemaking business, Grimshaw was fortuitously apprenticed to a private carrier business.[284]

When the railway from Leeds to London was completed in 1840, he became superintendent of goods at several of its branches. At this time, he met Eliza Maria Topham in the Baptist Church choir. A professional singer, she once appeared by request before Queen Victoria. The couple was drawn to the Second Advent Doctrine out of America and then to the preaching of the Latter-day Saints.[285]

Arthur Grimshaw. *Courtesy the Jefferson City Area Chamber of Commerce.*

Jonathan Grimshaw converted after asking the saints to administer the ordinance of laying-on of hands to heal his wife, who was unable to nurse her children. They had lost three of seven children in infancy, and son Arthur was three months old at the time, taking a bottle. Afterward, Eliza produced milk.[286]

The Grimshaws were baptized, and Jonathan was ordained a priest in 1849. He was made an elder in 1850, and the family of eight, including his sister-in-law Hannah Topham, immigrated to America aboard the *Ellen*, under Captain Phillips, in 1851, bound for Deseret. Named for the honeybee in the *Book of Mormon*, it was the provisional state proposed by the church settlers in Salt Lake City.[287]

In his journal, Jonathan Grimshaw noted passing Jefferson City in April aboard the steamer *Sacramento* and that "a noble looking building of stone stands on an eminence commanding an extensive view of the river." The sojourners traded water for wagon train at Council Bluffs, Iowa, to reach Salt Lake City, Utah, in August 1851.[288]

Grimshaw quickly became part of the ruling priesthood and an adviser to Brigham Young, but the lifestyle of the early saints was meager. Working in the Deseret Philosophical Society and in the church historian's office, Jonathan Grimshaw had high responsibility but low income. He is remembered today for his work sorting and filing the papers of Joseph Smith and assisting church historian George A. Smith to write the original history. However, Grimshaw had to tour with the Nauvoo Brass Band and serve in the territorial militia to make ends meet for his family.[289]

Disappointed with this experience after five years, the Grimshaw family headed east in August 1856 with a plan to return to England. Instead, they stopped in St. Louis, where Jonathan became the first agent for the Richardson Express Company and later its district manager.[290]

The Grimshaws arrived in Jefferson City seven years later, when Jonathan was appointed agent of the U.S. Express Company, a position he continued for thirty years. He served as presiding alderman for two years after arriving in the Capital City and then was elected mayor. His community involvement included Decoration Day planning and political leadership in the Republican Party after the short-lived Independent People's Party.[291]

While the Grimshaw family was in St. Louis, Arthur Grimshaw had the opportunity to attend Wyman's University before working eighteen years for the Missouri Pacific Railroad as a messenger between St. Louis and Atchison, Kansas. Later, he served as assistant postmaster in Jefferson City and two terms as Cole County clerk before being appointed joint railroad agent with his father.[292]

The younger Grimshaw was elected the first president of the Commercial Club in April 1893. His fellow original officers of this predecessor to the Jefferson City Area Chamber of Commerce included William Wagner, Rudolph Dallmeyer, Fred Binder, Joseph Porth, W. Ewing and L. Park. The organization's first objective was a Missouri River bridge.

Seeing that project through, Arthur became the first superintendent of the Jefferson City Bridge and Transit Company. He did not rest on his laurels but continued to work for greater transportation options for the Capital City.[293]

As mayor in February 1901, he met with Missouri Pacific officials regarding a direct line to Boonville, providing a short route to Kansas City. In 1885, he also had been among community leaders meeting with Chicago and Pacific officials in consideration of a southwest railroad from Jefferson City to Springfield through Rolla.[294]

Before the Grimshaws and before the iconic brick structure that spans the north end of Monroe Street, the Missouri Pacific Railroad first had to survey and lay down its tracks westward across the frontier. The St. Louis–Kansas City route taken by the modern Amtrak passenger and Union Pacific freight trains is the same as was originally laid down in the 1850s.[295]

The Missouri General Assembly chartered the Pacific Railroad Company in 1849 with the vision of constructing a railroad from St. Louis, through the Capital City and west to the Pacific Ocean. Chief engineer James Kirkwood surveyed that first leg of a challenging terrain.[296]

However, financial difficulties and time constraints caused the company to force completion of their product, cutting corners. Invitations for a great completion day were sent out in advance, creating an immovable

Moving Forward

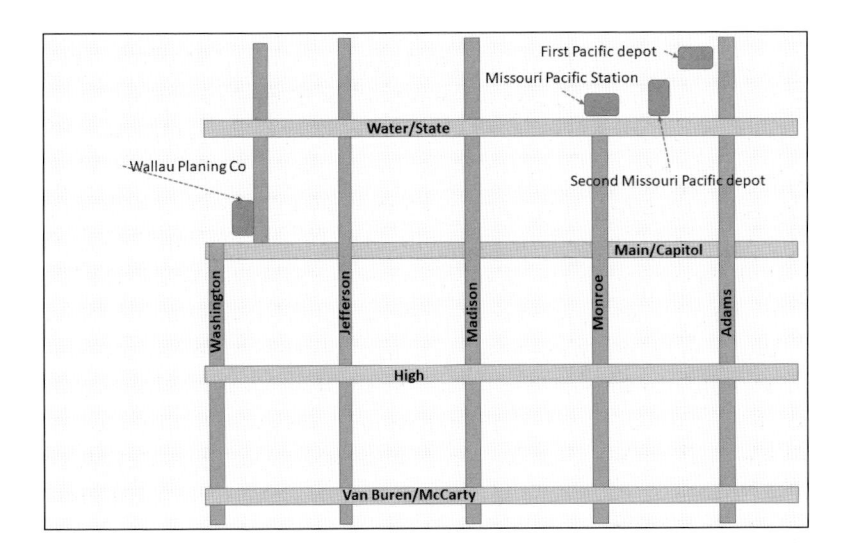

Map of locations associated with the Missouri Pacific Railroad. *Michelle Brooks.*

deadline in the fall of 1855. A bridge across the Gasconade River was rushed, with several parts of the deck not being fastened securely.[297]

The night before the big day, a significant rain fell, putting greater pressure on the incomplete bridge. So, when the fourteen cars filled with prominent business leaders and politicians attempted to cross, the bridge gave way. Even the morning paper of November 1, 1855, reported "some uneasiness has been expressed as to the safety of the road." The next day's paper reported, "The magnificent train of cars…is now a mass of ruins." The tragic accident resulted in thirty-one deaths and nearly a year's delay in completion.[298]

The first successful train arrived in the Capital City on March 12, 1856, traversing the 125 miles in seven hours. It was greeted by the original depot, which included a covered and gaslit transfer lane to the Packet line steamboats headed west on the Missouri River. The transportation advancement saved a traveler nearly thirty-six hours in a trip to the Kansas state line from St. Louis.[299]

The railroad line connected St. Louis to Kansas City in the fall of 1865 with forty-four regular stops. In 1867, Jefferson City residents had donated land in what is now the Millbottom for an engine house and repair shop, commonly referred to as "the old rookery." Eventually, a roundhouse and several other support structures and services were built on the north side of West Main Street, east of Harrison Street.[300]

For at least half a century, Jefferson City was a stop on a main artery connecting the nation. It connected trade like livestock, mineral deposits and local crops. It shipped the mail—up to sixteen mail trains a day in 1930. It sent soldiers to war, bringing many of them home.

And it brought people together, including the 1946 arrival of British prime minister Winston Churchill and President Harry Truman on their way to Fulton for the historic "Iron Curtain" speech.

II

BREAKING BARRIERS

The maintenance of Jefferson City as a leader in innovations and advancements was no less important after the Capital City question was put to rest, with the construction of the current Capitol, dedicated in 1924. Shortly after the limestone halls were erected on the south side of the Missouri River, chamber of commerce leaders were establishing transportation's latest invention on the north side.

The second Jefferson City Air Field was one of the first, and its flight schools were some of the best in the Midwest. The local chamber experimented with the first Jefferson City Air Field—little more than a mowed strip down the Gibler farm field, near today's Missouri 179 and Truman Boulevard.[301]

Seeing its popularity and future possibilities, Colonel Albert Linxwiler and William Tweedie led the chamber committee, which took out a ten-year lease from Paul Koch in 1928 for part of his farm, about where Turkey Creek Golf Course is today.[302]

By the time the field was dedicated in August 1929, the chamber had transferred the project to Jefferson City Airways Corporation, and the Jefferson City School of Aviation had students nearing their licenses. The field already was outfitted with radio equipment, thanks to a demonstration plane that had passed over earlier in the year, showing the promise of radio communication, not yet part of standard plane and airport equipment.[303]

Jefferson Airways under William Gundelfinger and Theodore Oberman started with hangar and service facilities for private planes, as well as future public transport and the Flying Boots café. Early flyers found the large, white Capitol dome a beneficial landmark.[304]

The second Jefferson City Air Field was located north of Cedar City and west of Missouri 63. *Courtesy Missouri State Archive Jefferson City Aviation School Collection.*

At the time, the expectation was that hydroplanes would become common; the location near the Missouri River was perfect. The proximity to the cliffs north of the field turned out to be a detriment, however.[305]

Taking advantage of the recently opened aviation convenience, Governor and Mrs. Henry Caulfield flew to Sedalia and back to visit the 1929 Missouri State Fair in a Curtiss Robin. The next year, the governor flew in the first goodwill tour across the state to promote aviation, leaving the Jefferson City airport in a Shell Lockheed Vega cabin monoplane.[306]

Just as today's municipal airport, the stop was a hub for celebrities traveling through or making an appearance. One of the first was Ruth Elder, a movie star and a transatlantic pilot who demonstrated her flight skills as part of the dedication ceremonies. The world-famous prizefighter W.L. "Young" Stribling refueled there on his way from Hollywood to the World Series. And the "marrying pilot," Ben Gregory visited in June 1934 to add Jefferson City couples to his list of dozens of couples married above fifteen hundred feet.[307]

Another interesting sight at the new airport was the emergency landing of seventeen U.S. Navy Sikorsky amphibian planes. The planes were returning to the USS *Saratoga* on the West Coast after participating in maneuvers in Cleveland, Ohio. A night storm forced them to turn back from Sedalia to land at the Jefferson City Air Field. Lieutenant Commander Wick praised the local airport's ground crew for its work throughout the night, refueling all of the military aircraft with more than one thousand gallons.[308]

The flight school also was a big coup, allowing the airfield to keep up with commercial aeronautic developments and attracting new business options. Cecil Bowman, a traffic officer, was the first local student to enroll. He was followed by hundreds of others, including Victor Raithel.[309]

Born in Jefferson City, Raithel was a driver for Weber Ice Cream Company when he began his flight lessons. From the beginning, he showed an "unusual aptitude in handling of a ship," an August 1929 newspaper said. With his wife, Bess, he moved to St. Louis and Indianapolis, Indiana, to earn licenses as a transport pilot and mechanical expert. And in February 1932, less than three years after his first lesson and at age twenty, he was manager of the Jefferson City Air Field.[310]

Raithel left the airport to operate the Capitol Cab Service after a terrible crash in July 1937. A plane he was stunting in went into a tailspin and fell into a cornfield. His injuries included a skull fracture, broken right collarbone, broken right upper arm, compound fracture of the lower left arm, fracture of the right thigh, fracture of the right foot and multiple broken ribs.[311]

The first crash may have involved Jefferson City aviator Dorsey Jordan in June 1931. Two passengers, H.L. Burnett and Frank Stephens, were injured when Jordan was tuning up the plane for a flight to New York the next day. The plane, owned by California businessman Frank Peck, wrecked in a field seven miles from Mokane.[312]

Airfield officials wanted to prohibit news of further wrecks and wrongs, fearing that bad publicity about accidents would give the field a bad name or hurt the industry. Such was the case the following month, in July 1931, when a Douglas bomber landed nose first, over-bounced and settled on its back.[313]

The National Guard airplane was arriving to take highway patrol chief engineer T.B. Cutler to Camp Clark at Nevada. The field attendants at first denied that a wreck had occurred, but a newspaper reporter happened to be at the field at the time. So, the field then reported slight damage and that the ship had proceeded on to Nevada. After another newsman's investigation, the plane was found still in the middle of the field on its back.[314]

Despite being a popular stop and a well-kept location, the Jefferson City Air Field was not a moneymaker. The chamber considered several funding supports, including construction of a canning factory.[315]

The Robertson Aircraft Corporation of St. Louis, owned by William Robertson, took a one-year lease on the local airfield in the spring of 1938. At the same time, the airfield observed the first National Air Mail Week with the support of Colonel Albert Linxwiler, who had originally led the chamber committee to establish an airfield.[316]

Linxwiler had served with the First Illinois Infantry in the Spanish-American War, including the Santiago campaign in Cuba. He joined the Missouri National Guard as an infantry captain in 1909 in Nevada, Missouri, and then moved to Jefferson City in 1913 with an appointment as chief clerk to the adjutant general. As a major, he served in Texas during the Mexican Border War in 1916.[317]

After deploying with the Missouri 140th Infantry Regiment to Europe during World War I, he was assigned to other leadership duties while there, including at the Meuse-Argonne offensive. Linxwiler was a founder of the Roscoe Enloe American Legion Post no. 5 soon after his return in 1919 and elected as its second commander in 1920.[318]

In civilian life, he worked for the Missouri Pacific Railroad before joining the adjutant general's office. In 1921, he helped reorganize the Cole County Abstract Realty and Insurance Company, serving as president. Linxwiler served as postmaster (1934–43) until he committed suicide in the basement of the old U.S. Post Office, on the north side of the 100 block of West High Street.[319]

John Randolph arrived in Jefferson City in 1938 on behalf of the Robertson Corporation. Under his watch, field operations went smoothly. In 1939, Randolph negotiated for the Jefferson City Air Field to be among the first sites for the Civilian Aeronautics Association's Civil Pilot Training program, working with the Jefferson City Junior College.

The next year, 1940, the local airfield became the only site for Civil Pilot Training west of the Mississippi River for African American pilots, in cooperation with Lincoln University. Randolph told the *Post Tribune* that the training of these pilots would be invaluable to future military defense.[320]

"No other nation in the world has ever enjoyed such a large reservoir of private fliers and private airplanes available for military use and training.… After all, the first 50 hours a man spends in the air is spent merely at learning how to look at the ground. These little ships do that efficiently, safely and many times cheaper than larger bulkier training planes," Randolph said.[321]

The Civil Pilot Training program was approved to build up the civilian pilot strength, as the United States anticipated entering World War II. The U.S. Army had only 4,500 pilots at the time. At the end of 1941, the training program had licensed 27,000.

Many of the local Civil Pilot Training participants went on to military service in aviation. For the White men, it was an easy road to enter as pilots or

Moving Forward

Lincoln University partnered with the Jefferson City Air Field to offer the first Civil Pilot Training course west of the Mississippi River, exclusively for African American pilots. *Courtesy Lincoln University Archive.*

ground crew in the U.S. Army Air Corps. But when the Civil Pilot Training program was established, the military had no aviation roles in its segregated army for Black men.

Dozens of the Lincoln University students who got their introduction to aviation at the Jefferson City Air Field were part of the barrier-breaking Tuskegee Airmen.

While Randolph instructed the White students, Malcolm Ashe trained the first class of Lincoln students. Ashe was the first Black pilot to earn a pilot's license in Washington, D.C., and, at the time, was one of only six Black flight instructors in the country. The *New York Age* called him "one of the most successful and unusual pioneers of Negro aviation." Before moving to Jefferson City, he was a flight instructor at the Flying Dutchman Airport in Philadelphia, Pennsylvania, where he taught Black and White pilots.[322]

The local airfield hosted five classes of ten Lincoln students before the Civil Pilot Training program closed, as the United States entered the war in full. At least six of these cadets earned their wings as officers in the U.S. Army Air Corps. And dozens of other Lincolnites, many not in the CPT course, trained at the Tuskegee, Alabama airfield as pilots, ground crew and in support services.

The first two of the Lincoln cadets to earn their wings at Tuskegee were Richard Pullam of Kansas City and Wendell Pruitt of St. Louis in December 1942. They were promoted first lieutenants while stationed at Selfridge Air

Field, Michigan, with the 332nd Flight Group, commonly called the Red Tails for the color painted on the tail of their planes for identification.[323]

They were among only the second group of African American pilots to see combat in Europe, providing cover at Naples Harbor for the Allied landing at Anzio Beach in 1944. These pilots first flew hand-me-down P-39 Airacobras and then P-47 Thunderbolts.[324]

In this latter plane, Pruitt distinguished himself as a fearless, though sometimes reckless, combat pilot. During his service, he was credited with shooting down three enemy ME-109s. One such event is featured in an episode of the History Channel's *Dogfights*, "Tuskegee Airmen." And in George Lucas' movie *Red Tails*, the character of Joe "Lightning" Little is said to be based on Pruitt.[325]

Pullam also was an accomplished combat pilot, rising in leadership while overseas. He flew more than one hundred missions, receiving two major campaign stars and recognized for meritorious achievement in aerial flight during sustained operations against the enemy. After the war, Pullam remained in the military, rising to commander of the 301st Fighter Squadron.[326]

The very first Lincoln cadet to fly solo under Malcolm Ashe's training from the Jefferson City Air Field was Wilbur Long. Already a student at Stowe College in St. Louis, Long transferred to Lincoln for the sole purpose of entering the Civil Pilot Training Program. And he left Lincoln after that first semester to continue advanced training.[327]

Long was the third and last Lincolnite combat pilot during World War II, flying a P-51 Mustang for fifteen successful combat missions. During the sixteenth, in September 1944, his plane was heavily damaged by flak while escorting bombers from Italy to an oil refinery east of Berlin, Germany. He made an emergency landing in Poland, where he was taken prisoner and held at the prison camp of Stalag Luft III, known as the setting of the movie *The Great Escape*. Less than a year later, he was freed with the armistice and was awarded the Air Medal Purple Heart.[328]

Most airfields and flight schools before World War II would not serve Black pilots, making the Jefferson City Air Field unique. Even the ground course classes were sometimes integrated, something not even done yet in local public schools. The progressive outlook of the chamber and the Robertson Aircraft Corporation provided an opportunity to dozens of African Americans in the Midwest at the time.

The local field shriveled after the Civil Pilot Training program shut down and Randolph moved on. By July 1943, the field had been abandoned and planted as Victory gardens.[329]

Part IV
BUILDING UP

Discussing the origins of utilities might, on the surface, sound dull. But the comforts and services we take for granted today were once risky investments for private businessmen. While other places in Missouri were talking about relocating the Capitol, the Capital City was working on improvements to keep it.

Before 1880, indoor plumbing, gas or electric power, sidewalks or paved roads were not seen. While the first Missouri River Bridge, completed in 1896, receives high praise for improving Jefferson City's status, the lesser-noticed utility ventures made the town more attractive.

Between 1887 and 1891, Jefferson City experienced an explosion of improvements. The Capitol expansion, the federal courthouse, a new state library, the prison warden's house and a new city hall were completed, along with another three hundred buildings. Four shoe factories were built, as well as three churches, two schools, one bank and a new industrial school that was added at Lincoln Institute, today Lincoln University.

As buildings and people increased, so did the need for new streets, water lines, gas mains, electric cables and telephone wires. Jefferson City constantly had to defend itself against criticism of being a backwater—not only in word but also in deed.

The leading businessmen in the decades leading up to the twentieth century had to pursue a vision of constant improvement, which could not be done without infrastructure.

Creeks and freshwater springs could not support a growing city. When the city's contractor failed to show up to build the first waterworks, men with their own businesses to run and families to support took the risk of buying out the charter, despite the construction costs exceeding the anticipated returns.

Reliance on a single person on horseback to light a dozen oil, then gas, streetlights each evening wouldn't cut it either. And it was messy. It took three tries for a gasworks to be established by these pioneer entrepreneurs.

Muddy streets were the norm for decades, carved from an untouched wilderness. Horses and buggies were replaced by early automobiles, challenging the city to improve its wastewater removal, surfacing and sidewalks.

At the turn of the twentieth century, communication was key to growth. Again, local businessmen stepped in to provide a better service than the nationwide company, with three generations from one family building an exceptional and influential telephone service.

12

Defined by Water

Without water, man could not survive. So too, without the Missouri River passing this particular cliff, the site of Jefferson City would not have been selected.

But it was the creeks, like Weir's, Goose and Gray's, that allowed the town to grow. Although these features were integral to daily life, they also could wreak havoc with flooding and posed transportation challenges requiring bridges and ferries.

From at least seven freshwater springs within the original city limits, the earliest residents could draw their water. One of these was located at the northwest corner of Jefferson and Miller Streets and was protected from public sale to benefit all in the early decades. Another spring flowed at the northwest corner of Jefferson at Capitol, where the Lewis and Clark monuments stand today. The spring that supplied residents in the Goose Bottoms, later to be called the Millbottom, was behind Mary Rogers' house north of Main Street and was protected with a stone wall and cover.[330]

Before the intense development of the street and buildings, the land between Clay and Lafayette Streets and from the river to Dunklin Street was dotted with gullies and ponds. Dr. Robert Young, in his reminiscences of the 1840s, said boys would float sailboats in the summer and skate in the winter on a pond in the 200 block of East Capitol, where the city parking garage and *News Tribune* parking lot are today. Another pond sat near the old Missouri Supreme Court building, at Stewart and Jefferson Streets.[331]

A windmill on High Street pumped artesian well water before it was declared a safety hazard. *Courtesy Missouri State Archive Summers Collection.*

In addition to city-installed watering troughs, at least one enterprising resident, John G. Schott, built a windmill on the north side of High Street for an artesian well. The saloonkeeper reached 1,400 feet, or the equivalent distance from the statehouse to the windmill site, before he hit water, requiring a pump and the windmill. For years, many used this well, believing it had medicinal qualities.[332]

Once a luxurious benefit, within a decade or two, it was seen as an eyesore and a hazard, having the large blades rotating above the uptown area, where most of the residents lived and conducted business. "During stormy weather, this windmill would run with furious speed," the *State Republican* said. By the time Schott died in 1895, water hydrants had been installed across the city and a public water system had been created. His son Emil spent several thousand dollars more than what his father's estate was worth to dismantle the towering structure.[333]

Some of the more prominent homes, like Fred Knaup's 1878 Italianate residence at the southeast corner of Adams and Capitol, were being built with indoor plumbing. The Knaup home featured an attic tank filled with water from the cistern.[334] Leads then ran into the four second-floor bedrooms. The leads also ran into the upstairs bathroom, which had a shower, a water closet and "douche appurtenances."

Building Up

Indoor plumbing, like most advancements, was a luxury for the affluent before it became available to the general public. Recalling her childhood growing up at 422 Capitol Avenue, Minnie Hahn Boyce, daughter of A.J. Hahn, recalled that society women were strong proponents for indoor plumbing once they discovered that the benefits included not having to pay for extra maid service when they entertained guests. After that, local indoor plumbing "moved with leaps and bounds," Boyce said.[335]

In addition to Knaup, other well-off families with early plumbing included the Tweedies and Ruwarts on East High Street and the Henrys at the southwest corner of Cherry at Capitol. These families were able to afford their homes and utilities because they had some of the highest incomes in town.[336]

Knaup, once a saloon and restaurant owner, operated the City Hotel. The Scottish immigrant John Tweedie operated a shoe factory with inmate labor. German immigrant Henry Ruwart was superintendent of the J.S. Sullivan Saddletree Company for fifty years. And Missouri Supreme Court judge John Ward Henry built his home across from the prison, where his son Jesse, a merchant and the state's first game warden, continued to live.

The Missouri State Penitentiary constructed a waterworks in 1878, but it wasn't until 1888 that a city election approved a public waterworks.[337] Densely populated areas across the state were becoming more aware of public health needs, including purified drinking water. Like many Missouri cities at the time, Jefferson City found it necessary to incorporate improved utilities to keep up with domestic advances, especially to remain appealing as the Capital City.

The city's terrain presented the greatest challenge to installing mains for a public waterworks. The hills were plentiful, and the limestone surface was difficult to cut into.[338] Although some cities designed and built their own systems, Jefferson City awarded its charter to Paul Bradford Perkins.[339]

Two years earlier, Perkins had received a patent on his waterworks system design.[340] He received several other patents over the years, including a self-lubricating car wheel, a safety razor, a hydrant, a condenser for steam engines, a hydraulic engine and a compressed air pump.

The Perkins design featured a water pump pulling from the source into a settling reservoir, which then elevated the fresh water to a tank, providing pressure to the main pipe lines.[341] "His propositions embodied the engineered certainty and technical detail that locally devised schemes usually lacked," Loring Bullard wrote in *Source to Tap: A History of Missouri's Public Water Supplies*.[342]

His system had already been installed successfully in Kansas and Arkansas and in several Missouri towns: St. Joseph (1879), Joplin (1881), Boonville (1883), Independence (1884), Nevada (1885) and Clinton (1886). For ease, Perkins carried a waterworks ordinance template with him when he met with city officials.[343]

Born in Maine and reared in New York, Perkins gained his experience as a hydraulic engineer in Illinois before moving to Springfield, where he founded the Springfield Water Company in 1883.[344]

Perkins had added his own ironworks to serve both his waterworks and the Frisco Railroad when he received Jefferson City's charter. At this time, he had begun a massive construction project for an opera house in Springfield, which kept him occupied.[345]

Jefferson City officials had given Perkins ninety days to begin the work at the intersection of Main and Brooks Streets. After sixty days, only secondhand pipes were to be found in the area, so, leading men including Frederick Binder, William Wagner and Jacob Fisher took over the charter from the city and bought out Perkins for $1,800.

Ironically, in 1885 in Clinton, Perkins was on the opposite side of a similar circumstance. The town had approved construction of a waterworks by a couple of local men who had done nothing in six months, and the contract was sold to Perkins.[346]

The Jefferson City Water Works Company Inc. was formed for $100,000 bond by Binder, a prolific builder in central Missouri; Wagner, owner of the Monroe House; and Fisher, attorney and journalist. Other board members included William Dallmeyer, Judge Walker, Joe Edwards, William Davison and Clay Smith.[347]

Born to a practical lumberman from generations of builders in Prussia, Frederick Binder had arrived in 1866 in Jefferson City with the skills of a carpenter and an architect, quickly gaining respect and notoriety. He literally built much of Jefferson City at the end of the nineteenth century, including the federal courthouse and post office, while he was superintendent of construction for the U.S. Treasury Department.[348]

He also built the present Executive Mansion, the 1887 Capitol expansion and the Merchants Bank at 101 West High Street. And Binder erected both the present St. Peter Catholic Church and Central United Church of Christ buildings.[349]

On the night of the February 5, 1911 Capitol fire, Binder was with Governor Herbert Hadley, examining the flames. Standing in the corridor, the governor urged several firemen to take a line of hose forward to protect the offices of the governor and secretary of state. When the volunteers said they were afraid of the walls falling on them, Binder assisted the governor in carrying the nozzle forward themselves. The next morning, Binder examined the results with the governor; he then was appointed to a three-man commission to assess the feasibility of repair.

Binder also was a preferred builder across the state, including the Engineering, Power House, Mechanic Arts and Academic Hall buildings at the University of Missouri–Columbia; the state reform school, Boonville; the lunatic asylum and the deaf school, Fulton; and the industrial school for girls, Chillicothe.[350]

By 1888, Frederick Binder had served ten years as city councilman and one term as mayor and was the first and acting president of the Jefferson City Building and Loan Association. Afterward, he would serve on school and library boards while continuing as president of the waterworks and the Jefferson City Bridge and Transit Company.[351]

The waterworks was not an easy money-making scheme. Securing the needed capital was difficult. The four miles of mains, the facilities and five employees amounted to $3,000 in operating expenses, in addition to $5,000 in interest on the initial loan. The city commitment was for $3,000, and the first private consumers added only $1,500. The revenue would not even cover the interest until the Missouri State Penitentiary bought in for $3,500 per year.[352]

In the beginning, the tower and pumping station at Main and Brooks Streets—one of the highest bluffs in the city—generated water no better than that pumped from the river. But it was a start. Then, the Missouri Pacific Railroad signed a ten-year contract in 1890.[353]

When Caroline Long Price died in July 1891, she left $1,500 to the city to build a public drinking fountain in memory of her first husband and the city's first mayor, Thomas Lawson Price. The *State Republican* wrote: "This is a piece of enterprise the people have expected from the city fathers ever since the erection of the waterworks."[354]

By December 1891, it looked like the city would not accept the donation. But, two years later, the city passed a resolution to build a public fountain, with an inscription, at the center of High Street and Washington.[355]

The Chinn Building on the Lincoln University campus was constructed with access to the city's water mains to support its industrial courses. *Courtesy Lincoln University Archive.*

A new water main expanded the service in 1891, reaching the twenty-five-year-old Lincoln Institute, which was adding agriculture and mechanic arts courses as part of the Second Morrill Act designating Lincoln as a land-grant institution.[356]

A steady water supply was essential for the new industrial arts building, another Binder structure, designed by A.W. Elsner.[357] The forty-by-one-hundred-foot, two-story brick building was named for Alexander Chinn, an African American board member at the time. Early courses focused on tools and practical training in trades like carpentry, blacksmithing and machine work. Students spent forty-five minutes drawing and at least ninety minutes on a trade activity each day.[358]

By 1904, Lincoln's industrial arts program had its first African American professor, A.L. Reynolds, and had expanded to shoemaking, woodworking, mechanical drawing, farming, gardening, printing and typewriting.[359] Some of their work was on display that year in the education palace at the St. Louis World's Fair.[360]

Conveniently located near the growing Millbottom, the waterworks became essential to industrial development citywide.

The waterworks improved its chemical treatment and sedimentation process in 1905. And it was ahead of the state, except St. Louis, when it installed a softening process in 1914. Continuing to stay on the leading edge,

Building Up

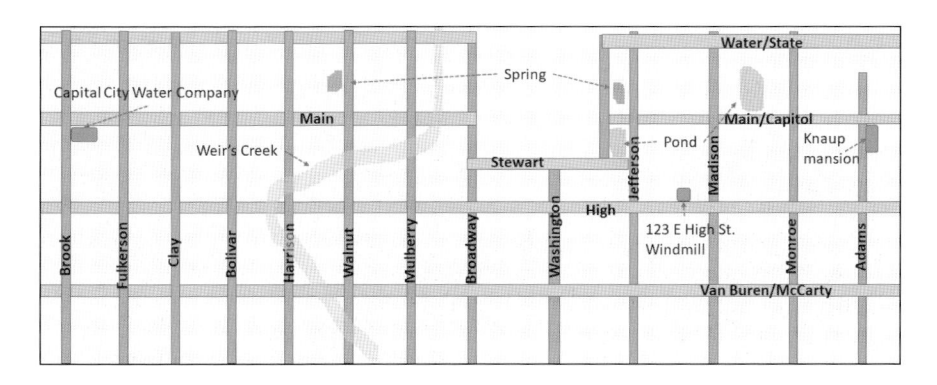

Map of waterways in early Jefferson City. *Michelle Brooks*.

the Jefferson City plant added a chlorinator in 1916, sand filters in 1926 and the state's first Dorr clarifier in 1930.[361]

Clean water anytime, anywhere in the city is commonplace today. It took foresight, infrastructure and forward-looking leaders to make it happen.

13

Gaining Power

Thirteen-year-old William Griffin used to ride his horse up to a dozen gas streetlights to light them each night. The young man, born to freed slaves in 1866, was the lamplighter. Even when the lights were converted to electricity, his horse, accustomed to the evening ritual, would delay Griffin's travels by stopping at each lamppost.[362]

Gas was an innovation in the 1860s, lifting homes and businesses out of the grime accumulated by the coal oil lamps and chimneys. It was followed only a decade later by electricity.

Griffin continued in the city lighting service for twenty-five years. At the end, he was involved in the rapid installation of gas lines for home and office heating. A coworker and another longtime employee, Mrs. W.L. Hager, remembered how Griffin would "doff his old derby and mosey out to the scene of trouble" as gas lines were being installed. Often, "Willie would be carried back into the office 'overcome with gas.'" But he always recovered, she said.[363]

The first attempt at publicly shared lighting came in 1868, when the state legislature appropriated $50,000, with approval for convict labor at $0.60 per day, to build a gas plant with the goal of lighting the Capitol and street lamps.[364]

After two failed attempts to organize a gasworks in Jefferson City, the Reverend Xerxes Xavier Buckner and Joseph Scrivner Ambrose gained the exclusive right from the city in 1871 to lay twenty-five blocks of gas lines. Their contract was for twenty years. In exchange, they erected fifty lampposts and laid nearly two and a half miles of pipe.[365]

Building Up

Ambrose originally looked at a site on the southeast corner of Water and Monroe Streets, opposite the Missouri Pacific Railroad depot. Instead, the plant was erected on the north side of West Main Street, west of Weir's Creek.[366]

"It is so pleasant to have plenty of light and so easy to get it," the October 9, 1872 *People's Tribune* said.[367]

When the lights were introduced on October 1, 1872, they were clear and brilliant, but the gas-lighting required users to understand that it was not like the oil lantern or candles they were used to. Several users experienced close calls before the lighting became common. More than once, hotels found unconscious guests in their rooms where the night before they had blown out the flame, as they would at home, not realizing that without turning off the gas it continued to pour into the room all night.[368]

The Reverend Buckner was the first president of the enterprise that became Jefferson City Gas Company. Born in Kentucky, he moved to Columbia early in life, becoming a well-known Baptist minister. He was president of the board of trustees and financial agent at William Jewell College while living in Kansas City. He died at age forty-three in January 1872, just a month after he and partner Ambrose received the city's go-ahead.[369]

Also a Kentucky native, Ambrose was the son of a pioneer Baptist preacher. He served in the Eighth Cavalry Kentucky Volunteers under General John Hunt Morgan in the ill-fated raid into Ohio and Indiana, where he was taken prisoner and held at the Ohio state prison in Columbus. It is likely that he met Buckner in Kansas City, where both were living before their 1871 contract with the City of Jefferson.

Ambrose also opened the J.S. Ambrose & Company in 1872. It installed gas pipes in hotels, businesses and homes. Gas pipes were laid to the Missouri State Penitentiary in 1873 and to Munichberg by 1876.[370]

In 1883, Ambrose moved to Springfield, Missouri, where he erected the first gas plant there and served as president for several years. He also was hired to install gasworks in Hot Springs, Arkansas, and Lexington, Missouri.[371]

During his time in Jefferson City, Ambrose promoted railroads, merged the two baggage transfer companies into one, worked as an attorney and served as the first president of the Jefferson City Chess Club when it formed in 1875.[372]

Despite his Confederate military service, he was named with several other prominent White businessmen in a thank-you ad from the African American community for liberal contributions toward their purchase of ground for Hedge Grove Cemetery.[373]

At the installment of the power venture, Ambrose was assisted by gas engineer C.H. Boyle, who drew the plans and superintended the machinery installation. Ambrose was secretary and superintendent of the facility from 1871 to 1876, when he was elected president. After Buckner's unexpected death, Captain J.L. Stephens of Boonville served as president, and local newspaperman James E. Carter was vice-president.[374]

Carter operated a retail room on the south side of the 100 block of East High Street until 1867. He then partnered with James Regan to buy the *Tribune* in 1871, receiving the state printing contract in 1874. Carter served with Ambrose on the Jefferson City, Lebanon and Southwest Railroad board of directors and as mayor in 1877. He also earned the place of Missouri Free Mason Grand High Priest.[375]

After fourteen years of growing gas services, a new power player entered the scene. The Wagner-Fisher Electric Light Company Inc. started with $10,000 from hotel operator William "Billy" Wagner, $8,000 from attorney and newspaperman Jake Fisher and the remainder from St. Louis investor C.H. Parker.[376]

Incorporating on December 24, 1886, the firm had electric lights in town by New Year's Eve.[377] Wagner alone bought four lights for his Monroe House, which was built in 1884 on the site of the Old Monroe House at the northwest corner of Monroe and High Streets. The New Monroe House offered guest call, fire alarms and electric bells in its rooms. It was an impressive establishment, with the city's largest sample rooms, where traveling salesmen could display their products, and a dining room known for its exquisite Thanksgiving meals and a menu including oysters, goose, venison, turkey, lamb, prairie chicken, opossum and pig.[378]

Wagner learned the hotel trade from his father, George Wagner, who operated a brewery and saloon and had opened the Wagner Hotel before the Civil War on the north side of the 100 block of East High Street, two doors west of the City Hotel. William Wagner also was a perseverant mining speculator in the area where others failed.

Wagner was the original treasurer of the Jefferson City Building and Loan Association, organized in February 1884 under Fred H. Binder, president.[379] Wagner also was one of the local assistants in charge of Governor John Marmaduke's funeral procession following his suicide in 1887.[380] And, he served on local boards, including the Commercial Club, the Southwest Missouri Immigration Society and the Jefferson City Bridge Corporation.

Building Up

After the first Missouri River bridge opened in 1896, Wagner spent $35,000 to bring his hotel up to the "high water mark of perfection," anticipating greater visitor numbers.[381] His wife, Lena Bohrer, was equally involved in the hospitality work. "It was the intelligent aid of his wife, rendered in overseeing the housekeeping and of that hostelry that aided materially in making the Monroe Hotel one of the best known in the state and a political headquarters for many famous men," the July 5, 1938 *Jefferson City Post Tribune* said.[382]

Despite his experience in the Union army and as county sheriff, Wagner was among forty-two victims of a twelve-day robbery spree in 1898 at the entrance to the St. Louis Union Station. The armed, masked men took a gold watch, thirty-five dollars and a diamond stud from his shirt.[383] While serving as Jefferson City postmaster (1903–11), his daughter Stella won the *Daily Democrat*'s World's Fair beauty contest, receiving a two-week visit to the St. Louis World's Fair.[384]

While Wagner led the electricity initiative, his fellow hoteliers benefited, including J.B. Kaiser, who invested in two lights for his magnificent, eight-year-old new Madison Hotel at the southwest corner of Main at Madison Streets. Fred Knaup bought one light for the City Hotel, at the northwest corner of High at Madison.[385]

The state bought three electric lights for the Capitol and one for the Missouri State Penitentiary.[386]

Other inaugural investors bought one light each. They included the *Jefferson City Tribune* newspaper office, 217–19 Madison Street, and Dallmeyer Dry Goods Company (208–10 East High Street). Three drugstore owners bought in: Dr. Nicholas DeWyl (231 East High), Dr. John Riddler (204 East High) and Adolph Brandenberger (130 East High). On Main Street, Jeweler George Porth bought one for his store at 212 East High Street and C.A. Ware for his livery.[387]

Abe Heim lit his clothing store (137 East High Street) with the new invention, as did saloon owners Isaac Bodenheimer (140 East High) and Theodore Schultz (236 East High). Grocer John Linhardt (302 East High), retailer Louis Wolferman (118 East High) and clothier Minnie Goldman (211 East High) also were among the first to light their stores with electricity. P.F. Myers and H.J. Gerstenkorn were original subscribers, too.[388]

These first lights had a limited use of between dusk and 1:00 a.m., due to the limitations of the original $18,000 plant on West Main Street, which depended on a one-hundred-horsepower boiler. After this experiment proved useful, voters passed a $75,000 bond the next year, and the gas and electric companies merged as Jefferson City Light, Heat and Power in November 1887.[389]

By 1889, the Capitol dome was lit by three arc electric lights, making it so bright as to be seen for eighty miles.[390]

The Missouri State Penitentiary built its own electric light plant before 1891, and the permanent seat of government commission considered leaving the local power company for an exclusively state-operated power system. State treasurer Edward Nolan suggested that it would be a small expense to set up and that maintenance would be minimal from the prison. After researching the issue, the state committee found it impractical to supply power from the prison and the expense too great to put in and maintain its own plant. In August 1891, the local company received a contract to supply incandescent and arc electricity to the statehouse, the supreme court building and library, the armory and the Executive Mansion.[391]

On the Capitol grounds, 6 arc lights were installed; 360 incandescent lights were installed across the state's properties. (The high-intensity, low-voltage arc electricity was the first to be used for commercial lighting, but today it is mostly limited to industrial uses.) In exchange, the state paid $1,950 per year to the local company; this amount was still $600 less than what it had paid annually for gas service.[392]

To fulfill the order, the local power company invested $15,000 in a dedicated plant. Its capacity of 135 horsepower was produced from a massive 50-horsepower Otto gas engine, combined with two steam engines at 35 and 50 horsepower. The improvements put Jefferson City "way ahead of all towns in this state of double its population," the *State Republican* said.[393]

The next year, 1892, the city council passed a spring ordinance to light the city until 1:00 a.m., which failed to gain the two-third voter ratification. No doubt, the state government's contract had influence on the city voters, who nearly unanimously approved in November the eight-year contract to power thirty lights at two thousand candlepower all night. The cost was $102 per year per light, which came to only $700 above the previous annual costs to light only until 11:00 p.m. with gas lights for only two-thirds of the year.[394]

Part of the electric company's early success can be attributed to Charles Hess, superintendent of the gas and light company. He conducted the company's affairs from his own plumbing business office, a storeroom at the corner of Washington and High Streets. He worked for the company from

The Jefferson City Gas Company and Wagner-Fisher Electric Company occupied the site on West Main Street, which became Missouri Power and Light. *Courtesy the Missouri State Archive Summers Collection.*

its beginning, until his unexpected death in 1904, just before the company was sold to a Chicago syndicate for $80,000 and became the Jefferson City Gas Light Company.[395]

In those eighteen years, he kept only a single journal of the business' accounts. Neither the subscribers' names nor the meter locations were ever written down. At least Hess' nephew Ernest W. Decker III remained with the company for some continuity.[396]

Hess had emigrated from Hessen, graduated with a law degree from Harvard University and was appointed by Judge Arnold Krekel to the Jefferson City office of the U.S. Register of Bankruptcy. Before the electric company formed, Hess was president of the Jefferson City Bank, which opened in 1874 with Gerhard Dulle as vice-president and William Boone and Daniel Boone as cashiers.[397] He married Ottillia Bruns, daughter of former mayor Dr. Bernard Bruns.

As a graduate of the St. Louis Teachers Normal School and a former teacher, Ottillia was a civic leader, serving as the first president of the parent-teacher association, a charter member of the Tuesday Literary Club and among the first public library board members.

The Hess couple lived in a handsome residence in the 900 block of West Main Street, across from the water tower. Here they also boarded Ernest William Decker III, the son of Ottillia Bruns's widowed sister, Effie. Decker had left his studies of engineering at the University of Missouri–Columbia in 1897 to help his uncle manage the company. The son of a St. Louis lawyer and a schoolteacher, William Decker followed his uncle as superintendent of the electric company for six years while also operating the plumbing company out of 117 East High Street.[398]

William Decker then opened the first Dodge Brothers Motor Cars dealership in Jefferson City at 103 West High Street and also operated the Capital Garage.[399] Later, he added Chrysler cars to his lineup. Krafft Motor Company of Washington, Missouri, took over the two car sales franchises in 1930, but Decker kept his garage and repair department. The dealerships and William Decker's garage facility relocated from the site in January 1935 to make way for Ed and Barney Dubinsky's playhouse.[400]

Decker became a notable figure in the promotion of road improvements, including seventeen years as a special road district commissioner for the county. His efforts are credited with the development of state Route 50 and the 1922 completion of the Osage River bridge, designed by Waddell and Son out of Kansas City.[401]

In the community, William Decker served twenty-five years as the president of the Capital City Building and Loan Association, organized in 1886. The organization "has been a friend of the young builder. Its officials are convinced that the wise newlyweds are those who start early in life to own their own home," the January 29, 1938 edition of the *Daily Capital News* said. Decker also owned 222 West McCarty Street, which he rented as apartments for more than three decades. From 1875 to 1903, the pre–Civil War residence had been the African American schoolhouse.[402]

Electricity became more popular and found broader uses. By 1907, white-lighted signs dotted the streets. And stage shows discovered the benefits for effects of electric lighting, which could also overload the plant's capacity. Electric company employees would request aisle seats at these shows so they could slip out quickly if they needed to fix a fuse or a wire.[403]

The local electric company was sold again in 1912 to the McKinley Corporation, which bought the Jefferson City Bridge and Transit Company

Building Up

Missouri Power and Light operated at the West Main Street location, where the Wagner-Fisher Electric Company started the first public electricity plant. *Courtesy Ameren Missouri.*

and later added the city streetcar system. As electricity became more a part of everyday life, local power companies merged to form conglomerates. Demand for more power grew with the development of conveniences, such as in the 1940s with electric appliances, televisions in the '50s and air-conditioning in the '60s.[404]

Jefferson City Light, Heat and Power Company and the Jefferson City Bridge and Transit Company merged with eight other power companies in north and central Missouri to become Missouri Power and Light Company in March 1924. The oldest of the group, the Jefferson City plant, was remodeled in 1927, and the bridge company was sold to become toll-free.

Two years later, the local plant saw major construction again, and it bought the old Dulle Mill for a garage and storage. The corporate offices relocated from Kansas City to Jefferson City in 1934, and a fire destroyed the building where the local and general offices had been leasing. It wasn't until 1969 that the Ameren offices at 101 Madison were built.

HIDDEN HISTORY OF JEFFERSON CITY

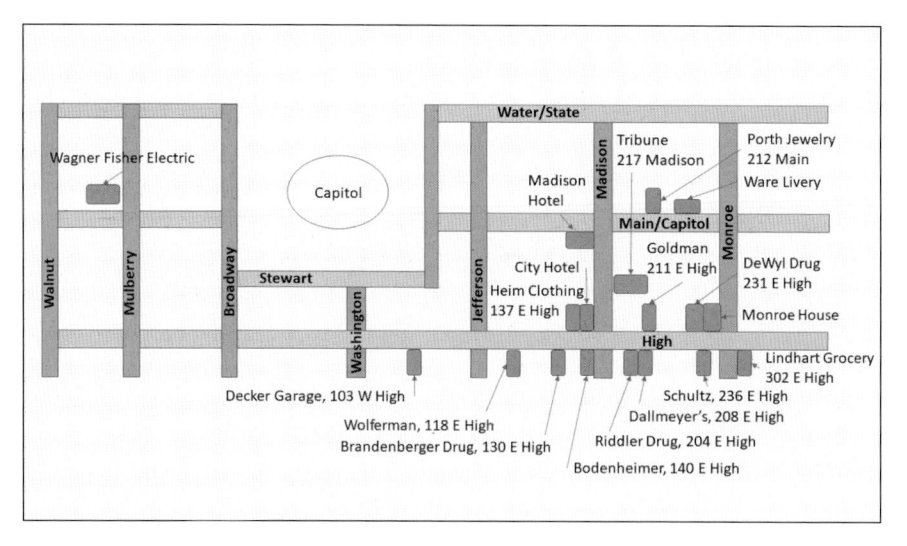

Map of the first locations in Jefferson City to receive electricity. *Michelle Brooks.*

A big push to provide complete electric service to state buildings began in 1952 with the construction of the thirteen-floor Jefferson State Office Building. In 1955, a new substation was added to serve state buildings, and lines were added to the Capitol, the Missouri Supreme Court building, the Broadway State Office Building and the Missouri Highway Department Building.

14

Crossing Bridges

The hills and gullies of Jefferson City have posed a difficulty for nearly every aspect of infrastructure improvement. That is no less true for city streets.

Not even a footpath existed on the site when the seat of government commission selected this hill. Every street began as a woodland. The clearing when the trees and brush were removed was a dusty or muddy stretch, depending on the time of year. And, depending on the part of the city, it would get washed away during heavy rainfalls.

Planks, flagstones, bricks, macadam and concrete were all means to make it easier for a horse and buggy on the streets and for pedestrians on the sidewalks.[405] Bridges, some built better than others, also were a necessity to connect the Goose Bottoms, later the Millbottom, and the South Side to the Uptown district.

Mayor Cecil Warren Thomas was one of the main forces in the improvements of the Capital City's streets as well as other projects, particularly the first High Street viaduct, named for him. Nicknamed "the builder," Thomas was involved in significant property sales as a real estate agent with his brother-in-law Thomas Lawson Price.[406]

"The fact that Jefferson City has come out of the mud [to] the automobile and the determination of the late Mayor Cecil W. Thomas, backed by a citizenry that favored street building," a 1929 *Post Tribune* article said.[407]

Thomas was born in Jefferson City to a Union officer and a fourth-generation Bolton, one of the earliest pioneer families.[408] He grew up at 226 and then 507 Main Street (later Capitol Avenue), worked as a clerk at the Missouri River Commission and was president of the Missouri Paper Box Company while building the Thomas & Price Insurance, Real Estate and Loans business at 200 East High Street.[409]

In 1902, he married Celeste Bolton Price, the granddaughter of the city's first mayor, Thomas Lawson Price, and also a direct descendant of his mother's Bolton family. Their wedding at the Price mansion, at the southwest corner of Washington at High Streets, was the last social function at the city's most opulent home before it was razed to make way for the Missouri State Supreme Court building. The Thomases lived with widow Ada Price at 428 Capitol Avenue, where the Missouri Chamber of Commerce is today.[410]

Thomas was defeated in his first run for mayor in 1909, when he worked on Governor Herbert Hadley's staff. But he was then elected in 1911, 1913 and 1915. He failed in his bid for governor in 1915, lieutenant governor in 1916 and Eighth District congressman in 1926. He was elected mayor again, serving in 1923, 1925 (when he also was chamber president) and 1927.[411]

Thomas' first priority in his first term as mayor (1911) was to see a viaduct built across Weir's Creek and the Missouri Pacific railyard on High Street. Voters agreed 17:1, passing a $70,000 bond issue in December 1911, with nearly half going to the viaduct project, completed in 1913.[412]

The construction, however, was condemned thirty-six years later, when another bond issue was passed to replace it with the present High Street viaduct over Missouri Boulevard. Although Mayor Thomas died at the age of fifty-six, his wife, Celeste, cut the ribbon for that 1950 replacement viaduct's opening.[413]

Thomas also championed the streetcar and the first buses, snowplows and airfield. He also advocated for the Forest Hills development, a toll-free Missouri River bridge, the Missouri Hotel and a city sewer system. Plus, Thomas sought improvements to the city's fire, police and street departments.[414]

He also had the responsibility of hosting visitors from across the state who gathered to celebrate the June 1915 cornerstone-laying ceremony at the present-day Capitol.[415]

During his second trio of mayoral elections, he was focused on bus lines and playgrounds. He told the city council: "Jefferson City is growing and expanding and we cannot afford to be backward about needed city improvements. We must move forward, also, or our citizens will move elsewhere."[416]

BUILDING UP

Mayor Cecil Thomas championed many civic improvements in the early part of the twentieth century, including the Thomas viaduct, which preceded the West High Street viaduct over Missouri Boulevard. *Courtesy Missouri State Archive Summers Collection.*

"It was during his administrations that Missouri's capital city shook off her country-town ways and assumed both the aspect and the action of a real city," the *Springfield Republican* observed in 1923.[417]

Thomas also was a founder and the first president of the Jefferson City Country Club, building a tourist park nearby, and he twice served as chamber of commerce president.[418]

"It was an era of progress in Jefferson City. Mayor Thomas was the right man for the job and it was the support of the newspaper that made progress possible," longtime news reporter Lawrence Lutkewitte wrote.[419]

Thomas' viaduct and other efforts were significant for their time. But they were built on the shoulders of earlier, more rugged efforts to accommodate the many visitors to the Capital City, as well as the growing businesses and residents.

The original street grid drawn in 1823 was only three blocks deep and eleven wide. When the town board formed in 1826, its first action was an ordinance designating streets in Jefferson City. The east–west streets were named Water, Main and High. The north–south streets were Clay, Bolivar, Harrison, Walnut (today Missouri Boulevard), Mulberry, Broadway, Washington, Jefferson, Madison, Monroe and Adams.[420]

Madison Street was the first to be cleared for commercial development, in preparation of the general assembly's arrival. The statehouse, a tavern and inn, the newspaper office, a log home and a store were built in the 100 block. And Jefferson Street quickly developed, with the riverboat landing at its north end, intersected by Water Street, which featured the wharf and the first jail, built into the rock cliff.

The most popular early routes were West Main from outside the city limits to Broadway, Broadway from Main to High, High from Broadway to outside of town and Jefferson from Water to High. Although Jefferson was a more popular north–south street, Madison and Monroe were the first two to be graded, along with High and Main.[421]

The city's board of aldermen took a wagon ride around the city to inspect the streets in 1876. The "only decent crossing" they determined was the one crossing Madison Street from the post office, then at the northeast corner of Madison at Capitol, to the old Executive Mansion, which sat near the northwest corner.[422]

As today, wastewater was a major adversary. Open gutters, loose rock and washed-out portions of the street were common. And property owners were called upon to make repairs to the street outside their homes. At that same time, city officials ordered two ponds in the uptown area drained, one between Commercial Way and Main Street in the 200 block and the other on McCarty west of Broadway.[423]

In August 1889, a visitor to Jefferson City noted that the city had only two good streets and one good wagon road. The first ended at the Missouri State Penitentiary (Main) and the second at the cemetery (McCarty).[424]

By 1896, the *State Republican* said the city had twenty bridges crossing small streams and about forty miles of macadamized roads and streets.[425] Among those bridges was a stone arch bridge on Jefferson Street over Weir's Creek. It was the oldest and longest of its kind in the state when it was removed in 1988. Dr. William A. Davison, who owned an entire block next to it, designed and built the thirty-three-by-fifty-foot, single-span bridge in 1857.[426]

The first pavement was poured in 1890 on High Street from Washington to Monroe. The first brick streets were laid in 1903 on High from Washington to Monroe, on Main from Washington to Monroe, on Main from Mulberry to Harrison, on Madison from Water to High and on Monroe from Water to High.[427]

In the decade before World War I, the city spent thousands of dollars to improve paving and sidewalks, which were made of boards, bricks and flagstones. Just as the horse-and-buggy roads were taking shape, William

Building Up

Dr. William A. Davison designed the first Jefferson Street bridge across Weir's Creek in 1857. *Courtesy Library of Congress Historic American Engineering Record.*

Linkenmeyer and Theodore Burkhardt introduced the first automobiles. A new era of street work was beginning.

The new vehicle was loud and smelly. It scared the horses tied to hitching posts and posed a danger if they weren't.[428] Nevertheless, Linkenmeyer, an engineer for fifty years with the Dulle Milling Company, was the first to buy one.

And jeweler Burkhardt soon followed with a Chalmers touring car. Ironically, two of Burkhardt's sons were killed by automobiles. John's automobile struck a Rock Island passenger train in Eldon, and Charles was struck by a hit-and-run driver in the New York City theater district.

By 1908, a trip by automobile to St. Louis could be made in fourteen hours. But that required improving state roads as well as city streets. The nation's Cumberland Road was a dream that began in the late 1700s to connect the East Coast with the western frontier. In 1829, Congress intended that the road, being built and paid for by the counties it crossed through, would end at Jefferson City.

Steam rollers were used to set streets at the turn of the twentieth century. *Courtesy the Missouri State Archive Summers Collection.*

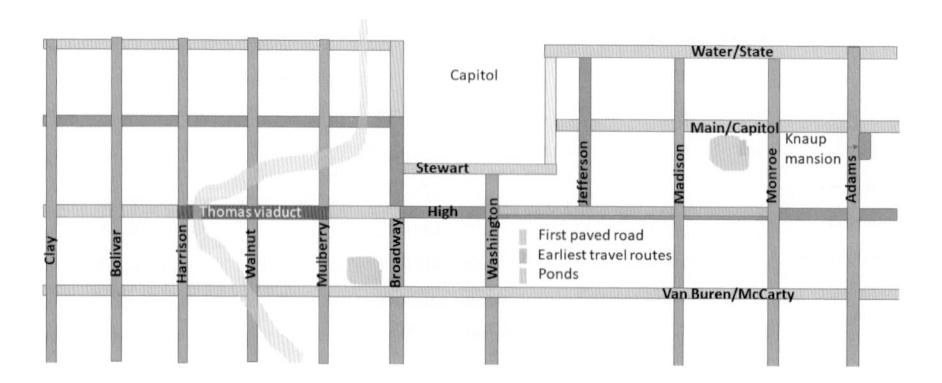

Map of the early use of streets in Jefferson City. *Michelle Brooks.*

Building Up

By the time it was possible, the Capital City was bypassed, the national road following the Boone's Lick Trail north of the river. In 1913, the only federal highway to Jefferson City was the no. 37 link to Fulton to catch the main highway no. 2, St. Louis to Kansas City.

By 1918, five state roads radiated from the Capital City. Across the Missouri River Bridge, roads went straight to Ashland and Fulton. One went west to California, another south to Eldon and the last east to Linn. A new era of highways had arrived.

15
LINES OF COMMUNICATION

In the field of local utilities, one family created quite a dynasty over three generations and seven decades. The telephone was the last of the local utilities to succumb to larger corporations. The McHenry family was part of the local phone company from its first day until its last, when it was absorbed by a regional service.

Not only did utilities have a growing community to serve, state government offices also came to depend on their business, too.

The Capitol Telephone Company organized in 1900.[429] The first stockholders were druggist G.A. Fischer, lumberman Ed Hogg, Judge A.M. Hough, lawyer Sam B. Jeffries, express man Houck McHenry, Millbottom doctor Joseph Porth (who would be elected mayor two years later) and Ed O'Rear, who was superintendent of the state insurance department at the time.[430]

The telephone patent was issued in 1876, and by 1878, St. Louis had opened the world's second telephone exchange. In 1881, W.B. Roberts established the first telephone exchange in Jefferson City. By 1893, this exchange had merged with the Missouri and Kansas Telephone Exchange at 202 East High Street, which became part of the growing Southwestern Bell Telephone conglomerate.[431]

This outside-owned phone system charged forty-two dollars annually for businesses and had about one hundred subscribers in 1900. The Capitol Telephone Company organizers felt that a local company could better meet local needs, starting with lower rates: twenty-four dollars annually for businesses and twelve dollars for residential service. The Bell local exchange soon closed.[432]

The Capitol Telephone Company's first office was on the second floor of the Exchange Realty Building, just east of the southeast corner of Madison at High Streets.[433] Henry Tyrrel was its first manager, overseeing the initial installation of more than one hundred phone lines.[434]

At the time, long-distance calls were made at the Bell long-distance office above the H.B. Church Shoe Store, near where Hawthorn Bank is today. A long-distance booth became available in the Capital Telephone Company office in August 1901, and in November, a toll phone was installed at the Missouri Pacific Railway Station.[435]

About 1910, Kinloch Telephone Company of St. Louis built a long-distance line from St. Louis through Fulton, Jefferson City and Sedalia and then on to Carthage and Joplin, providing direct service to Capital City users.[436]

In 1902, the local phone company reduced its board from seven to three, keeping Judge Hough and Houck McHenry and adding shoe man Lester Shepherd Parker. One of the first moves in the new reorganization was to raise rates, as the company was not making a profit. Later, Houck McHenry was named general manager and remained on the board as secretary-treasurer, with his wife, Thenia, as vice-president and Parker as president.[437]

Houck McHenry was born in Westport and moved to Jefferson City when his father, James, was elected the state registrar of lands in 1876. The family lived in the 800 block of Washington Street. Houck's own career began as a baggageman at the Missouri Pacific station, advancing to freight agent and then building his own transfer and drayage company. He was considered "one of the most thoroughly capable and popular young railway men on the Missouri Pacific system," the 1901 *Missouri History Encyclopedia* said.[438]

In 1904, Houck McHenry was named president of the predecessor to the Missouri Telephone Association, serving continually for thirty-one years. The next year, he was named manager and board secretary of the local company. Under McHenry's leadership, the company kept up with the industry developments, growing to 2,600 subscribers in 1920 and 3,600 in 1925.[439]

Lester Parker played an instrumental role as president of the company until his untimely death in 1925. Born in Massachusetts and educated in Chicago, Parker first practiced law in Kansas while raising livestock and teaching school. He moved to Minnesota, where he worked as foreman of the Kellogg and Johnson shoe factory.[440]

Arriving in Jefferson City in 1895, Parker began the Jefferson Shoe Company, associated with C.M. Henderson and Company of Chicago. He soon reorganized the business as the L.S. Parker Shoe Company. He left the shoe business about 1915, when he was named the first superintendent of industries at the prison after inmate labor for private business was ended. A respected, amateur painter in oils and watercolors, Parker was appointed to the Capitol Decoration Commission for the current state Capitol. And he wrote a variety of musical compositions.[441]

The phone company reorganized at Parker's death as the Capital City Telephone Company; Houck McHenry was made president and treasurer. His wife, Thenia Bolton, continued as secretary, and Parker's widow, Zue Gordon, was elected vice-president. Two director's seats were added for the second generation, Foster Bolton McHenry and Lester S. Parker Jr.[442]

Foster McHenry was five when his father got into the telephone business. The son earned a four-year degree in three years at William Jewell College, Liberty, where he also was track captain and played on the football squad. He earned a graduate degree in business administration from the University of Missouri–Columbia and returned to manage his father's Houck McHenry Transfer Company.[443]

Many sons of prominent Jefferson City men served in the 356th Infantry, Company M during World War I. Foster McHenry, the company sergeant, was wounded and gassed at Saint-Mihiel, France.[444]

After recovering from the war, Foster worked in insurance and then as manager of the Madison Hotel before joining the phone company as a plant accountant in 1925 and advancing to assistant manager in 1928.[445]

The phone company later moved its headquarters to the southwest corner of Monroe Street and Capitol Avenue, then to 315 Madison Street in 1909. It built a new exchange building at 317–19 Madison Street in 1930. The two-story, reinforced concrete structure was decorated with brick facing and terra-cotta trim. It was built with room to enlarge, set back from the sidewalk to accommodate landscaping.[446]

The Citizens Public Service Company moved into the 315 Madison Street location, which received a complete overhaul. This building (since removed) was the gunsmith store of Adam Hirsch and John Roesen before it became the newspaper office of Albert Kroeger's *Missouri Volksfreund*, created in 1876.[447]

The modern exchange building, when it opened in 1930, served Jefferson City, North Jefferson, Cedar City, Wardsville and 350 rural subscribers. It had sixty employees and underground cables radiating six blocks from the

Building Up

The Capital City Phone Company continued to expand its services and offices through the first six decades of the twentieth century. *Courtesy Cole County Historical Society.*

building and thousands of feet of aerial cable. It served 1,100 businesses and nearly 3,700 subscribers.[448]

In the community, the older Houck McHenry served two terms on the city council beginning in 1900 after being the Democrat's candidate for mayor in 1898 and fifteen years on the school board.[449]

Houck McHenry was Commercial Club president in 1913, 1914, 1915 and 1919 and helped organize the Jefferson City High School Alumni Association to support athletics, serving as its first treasurer in 1929. He also was president of Farmers and Mechanics Bank and the Missouri Central Building and Loan Association. And he represented Cole County in the Missouri General Assembly (1919–20).[450]

"He is a good business man, a splendid speaker and a cool man on his feet," the *Jefferson City Post Tribune* endorsement said.[451] Houck McHenry was a man of high ideals and staunch integrity, focused both in his business and community affairs. He was active in efforts to retain the Capitol and was involved in securing permanent locations for the shoe factories outside the prison.[452]

When McHenry died in 1936, his son Foster McHenry took over the business as general manager and his widow as board president. At the time, the Jefferson City company served sixteen thousand phones.[453]

Like his father, Foster McHenry was involved in the industry's broader activities. Foster became president of the Missouri Telephone Association in 1949. And in 1959, he was elected president of the U.S. Independent Telephone Association, which later named his father to its Hall of Fame.[454]

Foster McHenry was involved with the Oliver Buehrle Chapter no. 17 of the Disabled American Veterans and was elected the state DAV chairman in 1950. He was the first commander of the Roscoe Enloe American Legion Post no. 5.[455]

Foster McHenry served on the board for the federal soldiers' home in St. James and was involved in the planning and 1956 campaign for the Memorial Community Hospital. Today, Capital Region Medical Center's Goldschmidt Cancer Center is there.[456]

In 1920, Foster married Madge Waddill, who also worked in the company as a board officer and was traffic manager and directory supervisor. They had two sons, John and James, and the latter became a Cole County prosecuting attorney and then Ninteenth Judicial Circuit judge.

The older brother, John, continued the family's phone legacy after he graduated from the Missouri Military Academy, Mexico; earned a business degree from the University of Missouri–Columbia; and served in World War II and the Korean War. John McHenry joined the phone company, being elected to fill his mother's seat on the board after her death in October 1948 while completing his degree at MU.[457]

After fifty years of operator service and with more than ten thousand phones, Capital City Telephone Company switched to dial telephone. The friendly voice of a local operator greeting a caller was replaced with a dial tone. At midnight on December 2, 1950, workers began switching the phone lines at the Madison Street offices. Hours later, flames at the Jefferson Theater on High Street took out the uptown phone cables and the electric lines.[458]

"It was now a do-it-yourself project of remembering five numbers and dialing them correctly instead of merely repeating three or four numbers to the operator," Nancy Ann Hudson wrote in *67 Years of Service: 1900–1967*.[459]

When the company merged with United Telephone System Midwest Group in January 1968, John McHenry was elected vice-president and relocated to Kansas City.[460]

Building Up

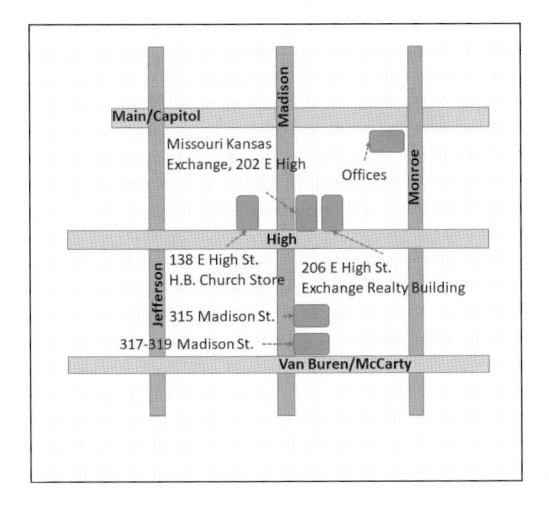

Map of locations associated with the Capital City Phone Company. *Michelle Brooks*.

John McHenry's community involvement included the board of directors of Associated Industries of Missouri, president of the chamber of commerce and president of the Missouri Military Academy Alumni Association.

In addition to decades of superior quality phone service, early in the technology's life, the McHenry family also left a generational home on Green Berry Drive. Houck and Thenia moved from 417 East High Street into the impressive city Landmark at 1427 Green Berry Road in 1907. Thenia's parties were well known. Foster and Madge McHenry moved into the Frank Miller–designed home, originally set on a hill with sprawling acreage outside the city limits, in 1943. Their son Jim lived there until his death.

Part V
PEOPLE AND PLACES

SOME OF THE PEOPLE and places that fill Jefferson City have changed over the years or been removed, while others remain. Regardless of the physical changes, the stories of Jefferson City's past remain as pillars of the present and inspiration for the future.

City government in a conservative town would have been hard-pressed to come up with the funds a century ago to build a city hall. The generous donation of a wealthy transplant made it possible.

The African American community of the early twentieth century took care of its members, crossing professional and denominational lines, through the vision of the Jefferson City Community Center. Despite segregation, it was a place supported financially by the entire city.

One person should have a limit on how much tragedy befalls her in a lifetime. That bar was high for Mildred Parsons Linn Standish. She outlived two husbands, three sons and all of her siblings. And yet she is remembered as a kind and gentle lady who served others with personal challenges.

These are but three of the amazing stories of Jefferson City's former residents and existing buildings.

16

Bragg Hall, City Hall, Henry Bragg and Joseph Clarke

The intersection of Monroe and East High Streets holds historic structures at each of its corners, not the least of which is the southwest corner, where the city government operated its offices for nearly seventy years.

Sometimes called Bragg Hall, sometimes the Tribune Building or old city hall, today 240 East High Street is home to the Cole County Abstract and Title Company. The three-story brick structure was part of the Bragg block, built by Gottlieb Martin.[461]

Perhaps best known as the contractor on the present Executive Mansion, Martin's contract business in the early 1870s also built Central School at Miller and Monroe Streets, did the carpentry in the county jail and worked on the lodge and walls at the Jefferson City National Cemetery.[462]

The state awarded Martin the $56,600 contract for the Victorian mansion with Italianate and French influences. It was designed by St. Louis architects George Ingham Barnett and Alfred Piquenard in 1871.[463]

Born in Wurtemberg and a housebuilder in St. Louis before the Civil War, Martin arrived in Jefferson City in 1865 as the superintendent of a short-lived manufacturing firm, Meyberg & Wanglein. The local IOOF Lodge no. 37 described him as amiable with a "hand always opened to relieve distress and affliction" when he died at age fifty in 1873.[464]

Martin's last job may have been the corner office building and performance hall for Henry Bragg. The fourth floor of Bragg Hall—the city's second performance hall—was large enough for seven hundred with

Built by Martin Gottlieb for Henry Bragg, the building at the southwest corner of Monroe and High Streets was donated by Joseph Clarke to the city and used as City Hall and for the fire department in the early twentieth century. *Jefferson City News and Tribune.*

a gallery to seat another three hundred. The performance area was designed by St. Louis architect John Thorburn, with scenery painted by Alex Wheatley.[465]

The city's first grand hall was built on the fourth floor of the Madison Hotel, which burned down in 1877, four years after being rebuilt on the grounds of the Schmidt Hotel, also lost to fire, in 1868, at the southwest corner of Main and Madison.[466]

Virginia-born Henry Allan Bragg died at age forty-one, only three years after this building was erected. A "genial gentleman [with] fine literary attainments," according to his obituary, Bragg was awarded clemency from President Andrew Johnson in January 1866 for his participation as an officer in the rebel army.[467]

Bragg bought the corner lot, with forty-four feet fronting High Street, in 1872 from the public sale of several lots along Monroe Street owned by Judge W.E. Dunscomb. Bragg immediately engaged Martin for construction. Major Joseph Clarke bought the property after Bragg's death in 1875.

Across Monroe Street in 1873, what is known today as the Democrat Building was erected to hold Christ Linhart's grocery on the main floor and the law office of E.L. Edwards above. Then, in 1876, south of Bragg Hall facing Monroe Street, Fred Knaup engaged local architect Fred Binder to build three adjacent stores with second-floor offices to meet the increasing demand for professional office space.[468]

The Music Hall, which holds Samuel's Tuxedos today, was built west of the Bragg Building and east of the Dallmeyer Building in 1883 by Frank

Schmidt. Originally, the Bodenheimer saloon filled the first floor; above were the offices of the Capital Water Company.[469]

Across High Street in 1884, William Wagner had the Monroe House Hotel and Saloon, formerly operated by William Mausehund. It was razed and replaced with a new forty-two-room Monroe House in the Victorian Italianate style.

The fourth corner of High and Monroe Streets held the Cole County Courthouse. During the Bragg Hall performance era, the third courthouse was in use, as the present building was not completed until 1897 by Frank B. Miller.

The performance venue was operated by a committee of stockholders, including Ashley Ewing, A.B. Thornton, J.R. Crow and Judge Alfred Krekel.[470] For its few decades of use, it featured home talent for fundraisers and church and school programs, as well as traveling shows. The locals counted on members of the general assembly to buy tickets when in town. Traveling shows that stopped there included Buffalo Bill, before his Wild West Show days, Milton and Dolly Nobles and Peyton's Comedy Company.[471]

The performance hall was threatened by a fire at Linhart's grocery in October 1878. Men with water buckets were posted on the porch (removed in 1890) and in Bragg Hall and the attic. Eventually, the roof fell in and mercifully cooled the performance hall. Responders saved the wagon shop and the blacksmith shop south of the original fire, instead of Bragg Hall, because it would have been more difficult, the *People's Tribune* reported.[472]

Clarke built an amusement hall on the north side of the 300 block of East Main Street, later known as the McClung Transfer Company Barn, where First Christian Church is today. However, the design of a performance hall over a livery stable proved to be unwise. "Folks never took to an upstairs opera house, when the first floor was a livery barn…whinnying horses marred the effects of the orchestra," the *Kansas City Star* said.[473]

After the Lohman Opera House opened in 1885 at the southeast corner of High and Jefferson, Bragg Hall's stage was removed and hardwood floors were laid for a skating rink.[474] The performance area later was converted to a box factory, where a fire broke out. The fire service confined the damage to the fourth floor, which was never rebuilt. Instead, Clarke had the new roof added to the third floor, and a fire bell tower was constructed on the roof.[475]

The lower level was occupied by the *People's Tribune*, operated by Joseph F. Regan and James Carter in the 1870s until the former's death in 1877. Carter sold it to Hugh Stephens and the Tribune Printing Company in 1880.[476]

J.E. Goetz operated a grocery at street level, and Willis Winston, county coroner, had his physician's office there in the 1880s. Before 1897, J.F. Heinrich, the "Furniture King," operated his furniture and undertaking business on the main floor. L.M. Walther continued the furniture and undertaking business there in the 1900s.

When owner Joseph Marcus Clarke died in 1889, he donated the Bragg Hall building to the city government, which at that time had its offices in a frame building on the north side of High Street at the corner with Monroe, basically where the street parking is today. Although generous, the donation became an obstacle to the city.[477]

The conditions of the donation included that the city raise enough money from rent to commission a bronze sculpture of Clarke plus life-size portraits of his third wife, Lavinia, and two sons, Junius and Marcus. Marcus, his only child from his first wife to survive to adulthood, operated a mercantile in Castle Rock and died in 1865 in Kentucky. Junius, the last of Clarke's twelve children to die, was a lawyer in Jefferson City until his premature death in 1878.[478]

Furthermore, the city was obligated to maintain the Clarke family Carthage limestone mausoleum at the Woodland–Old City Cemetery.[479]

The Clarke family's art pieces were supposed to remain in prominent view. At one time, they were in the front window, then moved to the second floor and then into an interior room. Discovering that they had been scattered and were dust-covered, Mayor Earl Jenkins in 1929 directed that the paintings be cleaned and the statue repaired, then a suitable corner "in a manner of respect and reverence for a municipal benefactor" be made in the clerk's first-floor office.[480]

"It is our solemn duty to honor and respect the ancestors who made our present civilization and progress possible," Jenkins said.[481]

The city occupied the building from the 1920s until 1983, when city government occupied the present City Hall. At first, the city fire station was

In exchange for the donation of a three-story building to city government use, Joseph Clarke asked for a life-sized bronze sculpture to be made in his likeness, along with portraits of his wife and two sons. Today, these pieces of art are displayed at the Joseph Clark Senior Center. Courtesy Nancy Arnold Thompson.

at 238 and city offices at 240 East High Street. In 1925, the city only needed the second floor, with the auto club on the first floor and Missouri Pacific Railway offices on the third. By 1930, they filled the first and second floors. As city government continued to grow, departments had to be located to offices outside City Hall.

For decades, city government wrestled with fulfilling the will and using the property for municipal business versus the need for a larger city hall. In the early 1900s, Mayor Cecil Thomas tried to sell the property, with the proceeds going toward a modern city hall that would have sat at 210 Monroe, where the *News Tribune* is today.[482]

After the property at the southeast corner of McCarty and Monroe Streets was acquired, an effort to sell the property in 1946 was met with a lawsuit by the attorney general and the Clarke heirs, to whom the property should revert if the city did not fulfill its part. Mayor John Christy in 1974 also was disappointed with the situation, as city departments were spread out across the city.[483]

The solution arrived in the 1980s, when brothers Robert and Allen Herman bought the building. The $255,000 proceeds went to build the Housing Authority's Joseph M. Clarke Senior Center. The bronze and the portraits have been displayed in the dining room there since its opening in 1987.[484]

John Linhardt, a contemporary of Clarke's, told newspaper reporter Lawrence Lutkewitte in the 1930s that the statue was an excellent likeness of the donor, capturing the "pose characteristic of his aggressive and aristocratic setting of his chin."[485]

Joseph Marcus Clarke left his home in Ohio in 1835 to join his brother, who was operating Illinois' third established newspaper in Shawneetown. Affected by malarial conditions, Clarke took up horse sales, traveling through Kentucky, Alabama and Tennessee before settling on a plantation in Amelia County, Virginia. By 1845, he moved to Owen County, Kentucky, taking up merchandising.[486]

By 1854, he had moved to a Missouri farm on the Osage River, near Castle Rock, where he was appointed postmaster and represented Osage County for two terms of the Missouri General Assembly. At the beginning of the Civil War, he returned to Owen County, Kentucky, where he published its first newspaper for thirteen years.[487]

Clarke returned to Missouri in 1874, settling in Jefferson City, where he helped establish Merchants Bank, as the largest stockholder and its first president for fifteen years. The last building project he was part of was the

The Merchants Bank Building stands at the southwest corner of Jefferson and High Streets. *Courtesy the Missouri State Archive Summers Collection.*

Merchants Bank building, at the southwest corner of Jefferson and West High Streets.[488]

The building opened in December 1889, just days before his death. Originally, the bank occupied half of the first floor, with a sandwich shop on the other side. Upstairs, the Commercial Club met in one half, and six offices lined the other side. The Masons occupied the third floor until they moved to the southeast corner of Madison and High.[489]

Quite a wealthy man, Clarke owned a lot of property in the Capital City, as well as in Chicago and Kentucky. Like most of Jefferson City's wealthy, toward the end of the 1800s, Clarke lived on East Main Street in a charming southern-style home on the northwest corner with Monroe Street.[490]

He also owned what was called Clarke's Row at the northeast corner of Jefferson and Main Streets, where the Governor's Gardens are today. The apartment building was razed in the 1930s, when the state bought the property.[491]

Clarke and Lavenia were among thirty founders in 1877 of First Christian Church. In 1879, the couple donated the northwest corner lot at Adams Street and Capitol Avenue for use as a meetinghouse for the congregation. Although Clarke stipulated that the building be completed in three years with his own donation of $2,000, he did not foreclose when the church wasn't completed on time.[492]

The church still holds a communion set believed to be donated by the Clarkes. In his will, Clarke left $1,000, directing that its interest go toward a pastor's salary.[493]

Following his funeral service at the church, Clarke was taken to the family mausoleum at Woodland–Old City Cemetery followed by the "largest crowd in Jefferson City's history ever to follow a funeral procession."[494]

17

Damels, Diggs and a Stone Testament

The African American commercial center, called "The Foot," was once a thriving, self-sustaining community. All that remains is the stone Jefferson City Community Center. A place where people of different denominations and professions could gather for the common good, it is fitting that this one building remains as an architectural tribute to the investment so many made into the social welfare and neighborhood strength during segregation and into the twenty-first century.

Today's building was the product of the Jefferson City Community Center Association, incorporated in February 1935 with the purpose "to serve the Negro citizens of Jefferson City in the matter of welfare, reconstruction, education, charity, recreation, social life and other matters conducive to good citizenship."[495]

The first president of the community center initiative was Lincoln University professor John Wesley Damel, namesake of the campus' technology building. The local community and the faculty and students at the university did not always get along. But Damel was one of the great bridges between the two. He taught science for more than forty years at what was then Lincoln Institute and briefly filled in as president.[496]

Damel built the two-and-one-half-story, brick commercial building at the corner of Clark and Atchison, 1015 East Atchison, today's Common Ground, where his wife, Estella, operated the popular Fairview Grocery. Damel built several residences nearby, and he pastored churches in Jefferson City, Fulton and Columbia.[497]

People and Places

The Jefferson City Community Center developed in the African American neighborhood of The Foot to meet social service needs. *Courtesy Jenny Smith.*

Born in Florida, Missouri, he was raised by his grandmother until he was sent to Chicago at age seven to work as a houseboy for General Phil Sheridan. He then worked at the Grand Central Hotel to pay for his advanced education—a bachelor's degree in 1887 and a master's in 1890 from Hiram College, Ohio.[498]

The idea of a community center was an outgrowth of the work of the Modern Priscilla Club, an African American women's club created in 1906 with the motto "life is too short to waste." During the Depression, the club used a small building at 608 Dunklin Street to store and distribute commodities. As the members looked next to provide hot lunches for schoolchildren, the community center idea was born.[499]

Women like Estella Damel and Estella Branham Diggs drew in the support of their husbands, who were prominent leaders in the African American community. Mrs. Damel and Mrs. Diggs each served a long time, as secretary and financial secretary, respectively, for the center's association.[500]

The entry to today's center is named for Estella Diggs' husband, John "Duke" Diggs, who was the association's vice-president and was in charge of the construction.[501]

Duke and Estella Diggs were a power couple, advocating for both African American civil rights and for Lincoln University's advancement at the local and state levels. They were leaders in their fraternal organizations, the United Brothers of Friendship and the Sisters of the Mysterious 10—at one time, these were the largest Black fraternal organizations in the state. And they were central to the success of the community center.[502]

The Diggs lived a block north of the center on Lafayette Street, a lot now underneath the Whitton Expressway overpass. Duke Diggs first worked as a cook but ambitiously opened his own business moving furniture and other goods with a horse and wagon. Estella Diggs earned a bachelor's degree from Western Baptist Seminary, Kansas City, and taught in Olean before marrying Diggs in 1893.[503]

Estella Branham Diggs. Courtesy Missouri State Archives Duke Diggs Collection.

She was church organist at Second Baptist Church from age thirteen and was involved in improving interracial relations within the Missouri Baptist Convention. In 1944, she became the first Black woman to represent the Second Congressional District Republican Party as a presidential elector and in 1949 was appointed to the city's first racial relations committee.[504]

Despite the oppression of segregation outside The Foot, community leaders like the Diggs found common ground with White civic leaders to work on several other projects, including the Community Chest. The idea of combining several benevolent organizations into one fundraising vehicle was first realized in 1925, led by the Jefferson City Area Chamber of Commerce. Among the first nine organizations supported through the Community Chest campaign was the Modern Priscilla Club. By 1939, the Jefferson City Community Center was a member agency.[505]

The first addition to the fledgling community center in 1938 was a playground, built in partnership with the local Lions Club, which was focused on improving and chaperoning neighborhood parks.[506]

People and Places

Then, a second building on Dunklin Street expanded social services and educational programs, such as serving lunches to public school students and providing kindergarten classes for children of working mothers, all under the direction of Lincoln graduate Mildred Rose. In less than a decade, the center had become a character-building influence and reduced youth delinquency.[507]

All along, the association was collecting modest donations from the African American community. The first $1,000 raised was used to purchase the land and the two small houses the association had been using. Despite being in the midst of World War II rationing in 1942, the association received the blessing of the Community Chest to make a community-wide fundraising appeal to cover the remaining $1,500 of its loan at Exchange National Bank for construction of the present building. The association had never made a community-wide appeal on its own before.

When the debt had been paid off by December 25, 1942, the association thanked the greater community for its support in a newspaper ad: "America is the only place in the world where a minority can ask a majority for aid and get it."[508]

The one-story stone structure was designed by Lincoln student Roland Cooper under the direction of Louis Edwin Fry, university architect.[509]

Cooper became an Eagle Scout while growing up in Springfield, Missouri, the son of a World War I veteran and a schoolteacher. During his time as a student at Lincoln, he helped university barber Hubert Washington, who was scoutmaster of the Jefferson City Negro Boy Scouts of America Troop no. 15. The troop organized in 1942, sponsored by the American Legion Toney Jenkins Post, held its meetings on campus at Damel Hall and had twenty-one scouts by the end of its first year.[510]

To celebrate the opening of the new community center, Mayor Jesse Owens and other citywide officials participated in a dedication on November 29, 1942. The next day, more dedicatory programs were led by the Negro Women's Clubs, including the Progressive Art and Charity Club, Civic Pride Club, OME Club, Needle Craft Art and Charity Club and Modern Priscilla Art and Charity Club. And finally, on December 1, the ministerial alliance blessed the building.[511]

The improved and expanded location allowed for dances, organization meetings, cultural experiences, social groups and children's programs. It was also a soup kitchen and a USO center for Black military personnel during World War II.[512]

For the first fifteen years of the center's operation, the association was led by president Charles "Lefty" Robinson Sr., who had been a charter member.[513] A well-known, left-handed baseball pitcher, Robinson's efforts focused on youth sports and citizenship. He also was a charter member of the local NAACP chapter, serving twenty-seven years as its treasurer.[514]

Robinson moved to Jefferson City from New London to work in state government. He first worked in Governor Arthur Hyde's administration, then was the first Black employee for the state workmen's compensation commission in 1922. He clerked for the food and drug department and the senate before working at Lincoln in the 1950s. He retired as a funeral director.

He organized the Jefferson City Mohawks semipro baseball team in 1922. The Mohawks played exhibition games with American Negro Baseball League teams, including the Kansas City Monarchs, St. Louis Stars and Birmingham Black Barons, as the professionals traveled across the state. The pitcher, known for his curve ball, was invited to pitch full-time for the St. Louis Stars in 1924. But he quickly returned to be near his family and to earn more money with his job at the Capitol.[515]

Governor Christopher Bond honored Robinson as the oldest charter member of the local NAACP with Charles E. Robinson Day on November 4, 1973, and in 1983, the city dedicated its bus and public vehicle facility, on Miller Street, with his name. Robinson's sister recalled that "It seems like the white people [in Jefferson City] thought as much of my brother as the black people did, and you don't find that just everywhere."[516]

18

Gentle Resiliency

O n Jackson Street stands a recently restored home featuring a keyhole entrance. Here, a woman of southern dignity who met too many tragedies for one life built a testament to perseverance from the funds of an admonished government.

Sarah "Milly" Mildred Parsons Linn Standish built the Queen Anne–style home at 103 Jackson Street before 1900. Her parents, Gustavus and Patience Parsons, owned the lot and much of the surrounding property on what had been the east edge of town. Her parents' blue clapboard and stone house at 105 Jackson Street, considered by many as the oldest remaining building in town, sits just to the south.[517]

When the Parsons family arrived in 1839 in Jefferson City, Milly was a toddler with five older siblings and two younger. The first Parsons home was a modest stone home near the Missouri River's edge, about where the Dulle-Hamilton Towers stand today, north of State Street. Then they built a grand home at the top of the slope, near Capitol Avenue. It was surrounded by spacious grounds, larger than a city block, and a long flight of stone steps leading to the river.[518]

The Standish home, a two-and-one-half-story structure of brick and scalloped wood, was built after 1874, when Milly Standish won a lawsuit against the Mexican Republic for the murder of her husband in 1865. She received $40,000 in Mexican gold dollars, plus $1,500 annually with interest.[519] She owned both corner lots of the 100 block of Jackson Street, facing Main and Water, as well as the adjacent lot on Water.[520]

The Mildred Parsons Standish house was built before 1900 on Jackson Street by a beloved resident, twice widowed and who outlived her three sons and all of her siblings. *Courtesy Missouri State Archive Summers Collection.*

Her father, Gustavus Parsons, orphaned at fifteen, had studied law at Monticello, Virginia, and served in the Native American uprisings. Parsons was employed for a time by President Thomas Jefferson, and the former president's nephews later lived with the Parsonses, even marrying one of his daughters, in Jefferson City.[521]

Milly Standish married Dr. Henry "Duncan" Linn in 1851 in St. Louis.[522] He was a Cole County physician born in Missouri who had studied medicine at the University of Virginia. Dr. Robert Young recalled that Linn also taught school in Jefferson City for a time, then died in Maries County.[523]

Augustine "Austin" Martin Standish, an accomplished civil engineer from Limerick, Ireland, arrived in Jefferson City with his brother Thomas while working for the Missouri Pacific Railroad. After the Gasconade River bridge tragedy of 1855, he became the company's chief engineer. He was described as a gentleman of education and cultivation and of fine personal appearance. The couple married in 1857.[524]

Before the Civil War, the Standish household included the young couple and two sons, as well as her widowed brother-in-law Meriwether Lewis Jefferson

People and Places

and the latter's brother Robert Randolph Jefferson, each with property in 1860 valued at more than $20,000 (or about $630,000 in 2020 terms).[525]

At the earliest moments of the Civil War in Missouri, Standish joined his brother-in-law Mosby Monroe Parsons in the rebel cause. Soon after President Abraham Lincoln was elected to a second term in 1864, Mrs. Standish packed up herself and three boys—Richard "Rich," age seven; Austin "Stan," five; and Monroe, two—and headed south to implore her husband to return home.[526]

Colonel Standish had already been wounded twice and had served beyond the customary three years. At Wilson's Creek, his horse was shot out from under him, and his pocket watch stopped an otherwise fatal minié ball. And at the Battle of Pleasant Hill, Louisiana, he was painfully wounded in the hand.[527]

A Southern sympathizer traveling in Union territory, Mrs. Standish could have met a terrible end, despite having a pass from Union general Joseph Reynolds for her to reach Little Rock, Arkansas. Instead, she encountered several helpful people along the way, including Captain Cabels, who carried the Standish family south on the Mississippi River aboard the *Niagara*.[528]

"In view of the fact that I had not asked any favors, good fortune meeting me at every point was most remarkable. Surely a kind of providence guided me to find friends among strangers to help me through the difficult places," Milly wrote later of her experience.[529]

Traveling across country, she stayed one night at the Bonnie plantation. The son of that family had been killed in a skirmish at the Moreau River, just outside Jefferson City, during Price's failed raid. The rebels wounded from those September 1864 engagements were taken to the Parsons home, where Mrs. Standish, with her mother and sisters, cared for them. Since she did not see Major Bonnie, he must have died in the field. Mrs. Standish was able to comfort the Bonnie family by telling them he would have been buried on the farm of her sister and brother-in-law, Green C. Berry.[530]

Three years since they last saw each other, Mrs. Standish introduced her husband to his youngest son when she finally found their camp. Milly fed her husband cake and coffee from home. Ever the gracious hostess, she treated all of the officers to a fine dinner with a ham from the commissary. She and her young sons stayed with the Confederate army through the spring of 1865.[531]

"She spent much of the time during the unpleasantness with her husband and brother and experienced many of the hardships of war unknown to most women," her obituary stated.[532]

Then, in April 1865, news of General Robert E. Lee's surrender to General Ulysses Grant at Appomattox Courthouse, Virginia, reached their camp. Milly's brother, General Parsons, decided right away that he was going to head south to find better opportunities, and Milly's husband chose to go with him. They invited her to go, but instead she tried to dissuade them. In June 1865, she returned north; the men went south.[533]

Austin Standish and General Parsons were joined by the Honorable Aaron Hackett Conrow; a former congressman from Ray County, Major S.C. Williams of Tennessee; and Dutch Bill, Standish's orderly from Callaway County. The John Wayne movie *The Undefeated* is loosely based on the final days of this doomed mission.[534]

On the evening of August 15, 1865, the Standish-Parsons party was attacked by a body of Mexican soldiers, who robbed and murdered them. General John B. Clarke investigated the next day to find the bodies of twenty Mexicans but none of the Americans. Instead, he found a trail where bodies had been dragged into the San Juan River. Soon after the attack, civil engineer Martin Van Merrick, who had traveled part of the way with the Standish-Parsons party, heard Mexican officers "boasting how they had killed him and his companions" while showing off Parsons' horse, coat and pistol.[535]

In later years, Milly Standish won a lawsuit against the Mexican government for the murders, receiving compensation, as did her nephew Stephen "Kearney" Parsons and the widow of Congressman Conrow.[536]

"Although crushed by double tragedy which came to her as the result of the war, and its subsequent financial responsibilities, Mrs. Standish faced the future with grace and dignity which caused her to be one of the most beloved personages of the city," the March 20, 1942 *Daily Capital News* reported.[537]

Widowed for a second time, and with three young boys, Milly persevered, first keeping the Wagner Hotel, then serving as matron of the Missouri State Penitentiary. For decades, beginning in 1875, she worked at the Missouri School for the Blind in St. Louis as the matron, then assistant manager.[538] Her sons lived with Milly's parents on Jackson Street, along with their orphaned cousin Kearney.

"[Her] rare executive ability is due to neatness and order observed on every hand….Her gentleness and uniform kindness won the love and respect of all the inmates of the institute and her presence in the building is a guarantee that all is well," School for the Blind committee chairman J.P.H. Gray told the Missouri General Assembly in 1881.[539]

By 1892, all three of her sons had died, as well as her father and mother and two sisters. Son Richard had learned the county clerk's duties from his grandfather and took over the job after the latter's death. He died at age twenty-seven of consumption. His obituary said, "He was a remarkably competent official and very popular."[540]

Monroe, who died at age twenty-eight, studied science and math at St. Louis University, later working as a clerk and salesman for wholesale drug companies.[541] And Austin became a doctor, working at St. Louis hospitals while his mother was there in her matron duties. He later moved his practice to Jefferson City to care for his brother Richard. Although he was appointed to a four-year term as prison physician in 1885, Dr. Standish moved to Colorado, where he died in 1890.

Through the 1890s, Milly Standish did a lot of traveling. She often visited her sister Julia in Lincoln, Nebraska, and her niece Nancy Berry D'Oench in St. Louis. She attended the 1893 World's Fair in Chicago and was chaperone for sixteen young ladies representing Missouri Daughters of the Confederacy at the Confederate veterans 1898 reunion in Atlanta. A newspaper described her at the latter event as "a sweet-faced, low-voiced woman in a dress of dove-gray."[542]

When Mrs. Standish's sister Julia died in 1908, she became the sole survivor of the Parsons pioneers to Jefferson City. She was a patient at St. Mary's Hospital during its devastating fire in 1919.[543] After being moved to the home of John Giesecke, Milly stayed with her niece Nancy Berry D'Oench in St. Louis until her death that May.[544]

She lost two husbands, three sons and all of her siblings during her lifetime. Yet, Milly Standish persevered through whatever life gave her. She braved enemy lines with little ones at her skirt. She took on demanding work that kept her away from her children. And through it all, she remained a quintessential southern lady with poise and a generous spirit.

Notes

Part I

1. Laws of Missouri, [1821] General Assembly, [1] and type [Regular Session], 1821, Chapter 351; State Documents Collections, Missouri State Archives, Jefferson City.
2. Lawrence Lutkewitte, "Early Settler Was Mayor of City 10 Terms," *Daily Capital News*, May 31, 1931.
3. Wayne Johnson, Callaway and Cole Counties historian, phone interview with Michelle Brooks. February 12, 2021.
4. "Commissioners Report" *Missouri Intelligencer* (Franklin), June 25, 1821.
5. Joseph Summers Jr. "History of JC to 1837," Nichols Career Center, fall 1987 class.
6. John Petersen, email to author, January 21, 2021

Chapter 1

7. "William Jones," *U.S., Revolutionary War Pension and Bounty-Land Warrant Application Files, 1800–1900*, www.ancestry.com.
8. "Jefferson City," *State Journal* (Jefferson City, MO), July 7, 1876.
9. Louis Houck, *A History of Missouri from the Earliest Explorations and Settlements Until the Admission of the State Into the Union* (Chicago: R.R. Donnelley & Sons, 1908).
10. "Jefferson City."

11. Gary Kremer, "City of Jefferson: Permanent Seat of Government, 1826–2001." *Official Manual*, 2001–2.
12. Darrell Strope, "Elias Barcroft: Surveyor of Jefferson City," Cole County Historical Society, Jefferson City, Missouri, 2021.
13. "Cholera at Jefferson City, Mo., *Choctaw Intelligencer* (Doaksville, OK), September 24, 1851.
14. N.A. Bedsworth, "Sale of Lots Financed in Part the Building in 1824 of the First State Capitol," Vintage Cole County Photos.
15. "Jefferson City."
16. Janet Ewing Boone, "Ewings One of First Families to Locate in New City of Jefferson," *Sunday News and Tribune* (Jefferson City, MO), January 17, 1943.
17. Hayward Dare Warner, "A Warner Family Narrative," Rootsweb.com.
18. *History of Cole, Moniteau, Morgan, Benton, Miller, Maries and Osage Counties, Missouri* (Chicago: Goodspeed Publishing, 1889).
19. Seat of Government collection, Missouri State Archive.
20. Ibid.
21. *History of Cole, Moniteau, Morgan, Benton*.
22. Seat of Government collection.
23. "Commissioners Report."
24. Chelsea Haynes, "Whisperer Remembered for Revolutionary Equine Equipment," KOMU, November 18, 2020.
25. Seat of Government collection.
26. Ann Stuart Dewey, "Basye Family Was Prominent in Early C. Missouri History," *Sunday News and Tribune* (Jefferson City, MO), February 3, 1935.
27. Seat of Government collection.
28. Ibid.
29. William Smith Bryan, *A History of the Pioneer Families of Missouri* (St. Louis, MO: Bryan, Brand & Company, 1876).
30. "Jefferson City."
31. Ibid.
32. "Another Old Citizen Gone," *Peoples' Tribune* (Jefferson City, MO), September 4, 1872.
33. Ibid.
34. Seat of Government collection.

Chapter 2

35. "U.S. Building Is Dedicated to Progress," *Sunday News and Tribune* (Jefferson City, MO), November 18, 1934.

36. "History of State House of Missouri," *St. Louis Globe-Democrat*, February 6, 1910.
37. *Missouri Biographical Dictionary* (Santa Barbera, CA: Somerset Publishers, 2001).
38. "Masons Slate Annual Dinner," *Daily Capital News* (Jefferson City, MO), November 17, 1976.
39. Nathan Howe Parker, *Missouri as It Is in 1867: An Illustrated Historical Gazetteer of Missouri* (Philadelphia, PA: J.P. Lippincott, 1867).
40. Jonas Viles, "Missouri Capitals and Capitols," *Missouri Historical Review* (October 1918–July 1919).
41. *History of Cole, Moniteau, Morgan, Benton*.
42. Ibid.
43. "Hotels," *State Journal* (Jefferson City, MO), July 7, 1876.
44. *History of Cole, Moniteau, Morgan, Benton*.
45. "Gordon," Folder #1115. Cole County Historical Society, Jefferson City, Missouri.
46. Ibid.
47. *History of Cole, Moniteau, Morgan, Benton*.
48. Ibid.
49. Dewey, "Basye Family Was Prominent."
50. Cole County Historical Society, "Recalls Jefferson City's Part in Politics and Civil War," *Sunday News and Tribune* (Jefferson City, MO), July 15, 1945.
51. Ibid.
52. Ibid.
53. "Local News," *State Journal* (Jefferson City, MO), January 23, 1874.
54. "Death of Hon. G.W.Miller," *Osage Valley Banner* (Tuscumbia, MO), March 27, 1879.
55. "By Balentine," *Sedalia (MO) Weekly Democrat*, April 23, 1874.
56. *History of Cole, Moniteau, Morgan, Benton*.
57. "The First Settlers," *State Journal* (Jefferson City, MO), July 7, 1876.
58. Ibid.
59. Terry Scurlock, U.S. Army, Register of Enlistments, 1798–1914, Fold3.com.
60. Bryan, *History of the Pioneer Families of Missouri*.
61. "Hiram H. Baber: Political Reminiscences of Half a Century," *People's Tribune* (Jefferson City, MO), November 19, 1873.
62. "From the K.C. Journal," *Macon (MO) Republican*, January 14, 1898.
63. Kremer, "City of Jefferson."

Chapter 3

64. Dorris Keeven-Franke, "Gottfried Duden," Missouri Germans Consortium, May 19, 2016.
65. Missouri, U.S., Western District Naturalization Index, 1840–1990. National Archives and Records Administration, Washington, D.C.
66. Jane Beetem, "Joseph and Elizabeth Wallendorf House," National Register of Historic Places Registration Form. U.S. Department of Interior, National Park Service, Washington, D.C.
67. Ibid.
68. Ibid.
69. Jackie Haar Trippensee, email to author, February 13, 2020.
70. Walter Schroeder, email to author, January 19, 2021.
71. Michelle Brooks, "St. Peter Church and School—136 Years of Faithful Service," *Jefferson City (MO) News Tribune*, City Landmark series, April 19, 2009.
72. Ibid.
73. Brooks, Michelle. "Father of Mid-Missouri," *Jefferson City News Tribune*, July 15, 2013.
74. Brooks, "St. Peter Church and School."
75. Ibid.
76. Michelle Brooks, "The Stone House: Landmark Believed a Gatehouse for Civil War Fort," *Jefferson City (MO) News Tribune*, City Landmark Series, July 21, 2013
77. Michelle Brooks, "Moving Story of History," *Jefferson City (MO) News Tribune*, City Landmark series, November 15, 2009.
78. Ibid.
79. Myrene Houchin Hobbs, *The Jefferson City Story* (Jefferson City, MO: Cole County Historical Society, 1956).
80. Donald D. Parker, "Immigration and Naturalization in Cole County, Missouri, 1834–1900," unpublished, Cole County Historical Society, Jefferson City, Missouri, 1945.
81. Ibid.
82. Ibid.
83. Missouri, U.S., Western District Naturalization Index, 1840–1990, National Archives and Records Administration, Ancestry.com
84. Ibid.
85. Guy S. Sone, "G.H. Dulle, His Home and Family," *Jefferson City (MO) News Tribune*, 1961.
86. Ibid.
87. Ibid.

Notes to Pages 34–40

88. Ibid.
89. "A Historic Personage," *Iron County Register* (Ironton, MO), September 12, 1889.
90. Laws of Missouri, [1844–45] General Assembly, [13] and type [Regular Session], 1844.
91. *History of Cole, Moniteau, Morgan, Benton.*
92. "History of Temple Beth El," Templebethel-jc.org/history.
93. Ibid.
94. R.E. Young, *Pioneers of High, Water and Main: Reflections of Jefferson City* (Jefferson City, MO: Twelfth State, 1997).
95. *History of Cole, Moniteau, Morgan, Benton.*
96. Ibid.
97. Ibid.
98. "The Old Building Corner of High and Jefferson Streets," *Jefferson City People's Tribune*, May 7, 1873.
99. *History of Cole, Moniteau, Morgan, Benton.*

Part II

100. Kimberly Harper, "Joseph Charless," State Historical Society of Missouri Historic Missourians.
101. "Old Franklin, Missouri & the Start of the Santa Fe Trail," Legends of America, www.legendsofamerica.com.
102. "Calvin Gunn" folder, Cole County Historical Society, Jefferson City, Missouri.
103. *History of Cole, Moniteau, Morgan, Benton.*

Chapter 4

104. "Calvin Gunn" folder.
105. Walter Williams, *A History of Northwest Missouri* (Chicago: Lewis Publishing Company, 1915).
106. Ibid.
107. Betty Collier, "William Franklin Dunnica," Howard County Missouri Biographies, www.usgwarchives.net.
108. Ibid.
109. Ibid.
110. Williams, *History of Northwest Missouri.*
111. *History of Cole, Moniteau, Morgan, Benton.*
112. "By Balentine." *Sedalia (MO) Weekly Democrat*, April 23, 1874.

151

113. *Jefferson City News Tribune*, July 7, 1946.
114. *History of Cole, Moniteau, Morgan, Benton*.
115. Williams, *History of Northwest Missouri*.
116. Laws of Missouri, [1832–33] General Assembly, [7] and type [Regular Session], page 208, January 15, 1833.
117. Ibid.
118. *History of Cole, Moniteau, Morgan, Benton*.
119. "75 to 100 Years Ago," *Daily Capital News* (Jefferson City, MO), November 11, 1970.
120. "Calvin Gunn" Folder, Cole County Historical Society, Jefferson City, Missouri.
121. Ibid.
122. "Died," *People's Tribune* (Jefferson City, MO), September 13, 1971.
123. "Our Home: The B. Gratz Brown and Upschulte Houses," Cole County Historical Society, Jefferson City, Missouri.
124. Ibid.
125. Laws of Missouri, [1873] General Assembly, [26] and type [Regular Session], 1873.

Chapter 5

126. *Boon's Lick Times* (Fayette, MO), February 28, 1846.
127. *Hannibal (MO) Tri-Weekly Messenger*, March 8, 1856.
128. *History of Cole, Moniteau, Morgan, Benton*.
129. Ibid.
130. Ibid.
131. Ibid.
132. Ibid.
133. "From the Boonville Commercial Bulletin," *Boon's Lick Times* (Fayette, MO), January 16, 1847.
134. "Legislative." *Democratic Banner* (Bowling Green, MO), March 19, 1849.
135. "Public Printer," *St. Joseph Gazette*, August 3, 1853.
136. "Public Printer," *St. Louis Globe Democrat*, May 14, 1853.
137. "Public Printer," *Glasgow (MO) Weekly Times*, February 5, 1857.
138. "Editor Dead," *Glasgow (MO) Weekly Times*, February 25, 1858.
139. "Another Editorial Muss," *St. Joseph (MO) Gazette*, July 13, 1853.
140. *History of Cole, Moniteau, Morgan, Benton*.
141. Ibid.
142. "House: Morning Session," *Daily Missouri Republican* (St. Louis), January 24, 1861.

143. "To the Patrons of the *Jefferson Inquirer*." *Weekly West* (St. Joseph), July 31, 1859.
144. *History of Cole, Moniteau, Morgan, Benton*.
145. Ibid.
146. Ibid.
147. Ibid.

Chapter 6

148. James E. Ford, *A History of Jefferson City: Missouri's State Capital and of Cole County, Illustrated* (Jefferson City, MO: New Day Press, 1938).
149. Ibid.
150. *Evening Missourian* (Columbia, MO), February 2, 1910.
151. "Charlton B. Corwin Dies in Jefferson City," *St. Louis Globe Democrat*, February 17, 1952.
152. "Democrat Seated After Hot Debate in Missouri House," *St. Joseph (MO) Gazette*, January 19, 1923.
153. "First Amateur Station Founded Twenty Years Ago and Club Formed," *Sunday News and Tribune* (Jefferson City, MO), April 21, 1935.
154. Ibid.
155. Ibid.
156. Kent Trimble, "Wireless History on East McCarty Street (Willis Porter Corwin, 9ABD)," *Electric Radio Magazine*, Issue 230 (July 2008).
157. "A Hobby That Led to National Service," *Kansas City Star*. May 6, 1917.
158. Trimble, "Wireless History on East McCarty Street."
159. "First Amateur Station Founded Twenty Years Ago and Club Formed," *Sunday News and Tribune* (Jefferson City, MO), April 21, 1935.
160. "Students at M.U. Operate Radio Station," *Columbia (MO) Evening Missourian*, September 16, 1920.
161. "Radio Broadcasting in City Began in 1922 with Opening of Old WOS," *Jefferson City (MO) Post-Tribune*, January 27, 1937.
162. Ibid.
163. Ibid.
164. Ibid.
165. "First Amateur Station Founded Twenty Years Ago."
166. "Jefferson City Overcomes Late Start," *Sunday News and Tribune* (Jefferson City, MO), July 18, 1971.
167. "Radio Broadcasting in City Began."
168. Ibid.
169. Ibid.

170. "Harry Snodgrass Record Collection," finding aid, Record Group 998.292, Missouri State Archives, Jefferson City.
171. "Remember the Schnitzelbanker? You'll Hear 'em Again on KWOS," *Jefferson City (MO) Post-Tribune*, January 27, 1937.
172. "Schnitzelbankers Went Over Big," *Jefferson City (MO) Post-Tribune*, March 3, 1930.
173. "The Dining Car Schnitzelbankers," *Gasconade County Republican* (Owensville, MO), January 8, 1931.
174. "Radio Broadcasting in City Began."
175. Jeff Haldiman, "Radio Station Marking 80th Year," *Fulton (MO) Sun*, January 29, 2017.
176. Ibid.
177. "KWOS Studios Feature the Latest Developments in Radio History," *Jefferson City (MO) Post-Tribune*, January 27, 1937.
178. "Tons of Steel Stretch Skyward to Form Antenna for Station KWOS," *Jefferson City (MO) Post-Tribune*, January 27, 1937.
179. "Pemberton Gordon, Manager, No Stranger to Capital City," *Jefferson City (MO) Post-Tribune*, January 27, 1937.
180. Haldiman, "Radio Station Marking 80th Year."

Chapter 7

181. "Edward H. Winter Dies in Rochester, Minn., Funeral to Be Held Here Tuesday," *Jefferson City (MO) Post-Tribune*, June 30, 1941.
182. Ford, *History of Jefferson City*, 290.
183. "New Home of the *News Tribune*," *Daily Capital News* (Jefferson City, MO), June 5, 1932.
184. Ibid.
185. Ibid.
186. Ibid.
187. Judy Ayers, Research paper 1964. Printed in *News Tribune* (Jefferson City, MO), October 11, 1987.
188. Ibid.
189. Ibid.
190. Ibid.
191. Ibid.
192. Michelle Brooks, "A History of the News Tribune," *News Tribune* (Jefferson City, MO), March 8, 2006.
193. "Durwoods Quit Field for TV Station Here," *Jefferson City (MO) Post Tribune*, May 6, 1954.

194. *Sunday News and Tribune* (Jefferson City, MO), May 22, 1955.
195. "Mrs. Goshorn Jefferson City Dies at Home," *Sedalia (MO) Democrat*, July 9, 1959.
196. Goshorn Folder #1006, Cole County Historical Society, Jefferson City, Missouri.
197. "Miss Goshorn, Social Director of Institute," *Jefferson City (MO) Post Tribune*, June 23, 1949.
198. Goshorn Folder #1006.
199. "'Jetty Jinx' Loaned to US for Coastal Patrol," *Daily Capital News* (Jefferson City, MO), June 23, 1942.
200. Goshorn Folder #1006.
201. Brooks, "History of the News Tribune."
202. Ibid.
203. Ibid.
204. "Special Facilities for Handicapped, Mentally Retarded," *Sunday News and Tribune* (Jefferson City, MO), August 14, 1960.
205. "City Committee Elects Officers," *Jefferson City (MO) Post Tribune*, April 12, 1950.
206. "Lost and Found," *Jefferson City (MO) Post Tribune*, June 13, 1929.
207. "Capital City Horse Wins Top Honors at American Royal," *Jefferson City (MO) Post Tribune*, October 21, 1942.

Chapter 8

208. Ford, *History of Jefferson City*.
209. Lutkewitte, "Early Settler Was Mayor."
210. *History of Cole, Moniteau, Morgan, Benton*.
211. Lutkewitte, "Early Settler Was Mayor."
212. Callaway County ferry licenses, Wayne Johnson collection.
213. "Ferries," *State Journal* (Jefferson City, MO), July 7, 1876.
214. Seat of Government collection.
215. Lutkewitte, "Early Settler Was Mayor."
216. "Rogers" Folder #1108, Cole County Historical Society, Jefferson City, Missouri.
217. "Jefferson City Steam Ferry Boat," *Saturday Morning Visitor* (Warsaw, MO), December 9, 1848.
218. Ford, *History of Jefferson City*.
219. Ibid.
220. Ibid.
221. Ibid.
222. Lutkewitte, "Early Settler Was Mayor."

223. "State Pro-Slavery Convention," *Weekly Brunswicker* (Brunswick, MO), July 21, 1855.
224. Craig Sturdevant and Gary Kremer, "Jefferson City Historic District Capitol West Millbottom," Jefferson City Housing Authority, 1982.
225. *Daily Capital News* (Jefferson City, MO), April 12, 1931.
226. Lutkewitte, "Early Settler Was Mayor."
227. Ibid.
228. "Laclede & Ft. Scott, R.R.: Branch Road Created from Lebanon to Jefferson City," *Bolivar (MO) Free Press*, February 2, 1871.
229. Dr. R.E. Young, *Pioneers of High, Water and Main: Reflections of Jefferson City* (Jefferson City, MO: Twelfth State, 1997).
230. Lutkewitte, "Early Settler Was Mayor."
231. Sturdevant and Kremer, "Jefferson City Historic District Capitol West Millbottom."

Chapter 9

232. *Missouri Senate Journal*, January 12, 1829.
233. Phil M. Donnelly, "Rural Free Delivery Service in Missouri," *Missouri Historical Review* (October 1940).
234. National Road, LegendsOfAmerica.com
235. Donnelly, "Rural Free Delivery Service."
236. Ibid.
237. *Traveler's Guide through the United States* (New York: Phelps & Ensign, 1838).
238. Cave Johnson, postmaster general. Letter to Thomas Hart Benton. State Historical Society of Missouri, March 20, 1847.
239. Ford, *History of Jefferson City*.
240. *Traveler's Guide through the United States*.
241. Ibid.
242. Ibid.
243. "The Mansion," *Sunday News and Tribune* (Jefferson City, MO), December 10, 1933.
244. Kenneth Winn, "Tour of Supreme Court Building," *Yesterday and Today*, Historic City of Jefferson, August 2011.
245. Young, *Pioneers of High, Water and Main*.
246. J.W. Johnston, *The Illustrated Sketch Book and Directory of Jefferson City and Cole County* (Jefferson City: Missouri Illustrated Sketch Book Company, 1900).
247. "The McCarty of McCarty's," *St. Joseph (MO) Gazette-Herald*, October 20, 1885.
248. Johnston, *Illustrated Sketch Book and Directory*.

249. "The Star's Centennial Edition," *Concordia (KS) Press*, August 11, 1921.
250. "Must Be One of the Oldest Inns in the State," *St. Louis Republican*, January 18, 1903.
251. Sone, "For Cole County Historical Society," *Daily Capital News* (Jefferson City), September 27, 1961.
252. "Metamorphosis of Historic Old McCarty House," *St. Louis Globe Democrat*, December 30, 1906.
253. Harry Norman, "Typical Antebellum Inn," *St. Louis Republic*, April 28, 1901.
254. "Metamorphosis of Historic Old McCarty House."
255. Ibid.
256. "Must Be One of the Oldest Inns."
257. Ibid.
258. George Walz, *Sunday News and Tribune* (Jefferson City, MO), May 2, 1965.
259. Jean Carnahan, *If Walls Could Talk* (Jefferson City: Missouri Mansion Preservation Inc., 1998).
260. Ibid.
261. "Funeral of Major Edwards," *Lexington (MO) Intelligencer*, May 11, 1889.
262. Norman, "Typical Antebellum Inn."
263. "Must Be One of the Oldest Inns."
264. Ibid.
265. Ibid.
266. Norman, "Typical Antebellum Inn."
267. Ibid.
268. Ibid.
269. "Metamorphosis of Historic Old McCarty House."
270. Ibid.
271. Norman, "Typical Antebellum Inn."
272. "Moon Restaurant Is Now Completed," *Jefferson City Post Tribune*, November 27, 1929.
273. Norman, "Typical Antebellum Inn."
274. Ibid.
275. "Will of Ella McCarty." Missouri, Probate Court (Cole County), April 16, 1917.

Chapter 10

276. Michelle Brooks, "Railroad Depot Connected State, People," *Jefferson City News Tribune*, City Landmark series, January 19, 2014.

277. Jane Beetem, "Henry and Elizabeth Bockrath House," National Register of Historic Places, Department of the Interior, National Parks Service, 2013.
278. *Daily Capital News* (Jefferson City, MO), July 22, 1926.
279. "St. Peter's Benevolent Society Observes 70th Anniversary of Its Founding Here," *Sunday News and Tribune* (Jefferson City, MO), May 31, 1936.
280. "Drops of Water, Grains of Sand," *Sunday News and Tribune* (Jefferson City, MO), March 25, 1951.
281. Brooks, "Railroad Depot Connected State, People."
282. Ibid.
283. Jefferson City Area Chamber of Commerce, Grimshaw Room sign.
284. Jonathan Grimshaw, "The Journal of Jonathan Grimshaw," FamilySearch.org.
285. Ibid.
286. Ibid.
287. Ibid.
288. Ibid.
289. Ibid.
290. Ibid.
291. "Died in the Night," *Sedalia (MO) Democrat*, August 31, 1897.
292. *History of Cole, Moniteau, Morgan, Benton*.
293. M.L. Van Nada, *The Book of Missourians* (Chicago: T.J. Steele & Company, 1906).
294. "Boonville Extension," *St. Louis Republic*, February 19, 1901.
295. Brooks, Michelle. "150 Years Ago, Missouri's Railroad Revolutionized Travel," *Jefferson City (MO) News Tribune*, October 3, 2015.
296. Ibid.
297. Ibid.
298. "Most Disastrous Accident," *Daily Missouri Republican* (St. Louis), November 2, 1855.
299. Brooks, "150 Years Ago."
300. Brooks, "Railroad Depot Connected State, People."

Chapter 11

301. Terry Rackers, interview with author, 2020.
302. "Local Airport to St. Louisan," *Jefferson City (MO) Post Tribune*, April 15, 1938.
303. "Jefferson City Initiative and St. Louis Capital Responsible for Opening Local Airway Inc.," *Jefferson City (MO) Post Tribune*, August 3, 1929.
304. "Air Excursion Thrilled 200 at Local Airport," *Jefferson City (MO) Post Tribune*, April 14, 1930.

305. "Jefferson City Initiative."
306. "Governor Made Fast Trip in Airplane," *Jefferson City (MO) Post-Tribune*, August 23, 1929.
307. "Noted Pilot to Give Local Enthusiasts Aerial Joy Rides," *Jefferson City (MO) Post-Tribune*, June 29, 1934.
308. "Amphibian Delayed While 17 Navy Planes Take Off from the Local Airfield," *Jefferson City (MO) Post Tribune*, September 5, 1929.
309. "Students Enroll in Flying School Before Official Start," *Jefferson City (MO) Post Tribune*, August 3, 1929.
310. "Student Aviator Dead, Instructor Hurt in Crackup," *Daily Capital News* (Jefferson City, MO), July 6, 1937.
311. Ibid.
312. "Jefferson City Aviator Dies in Plane Crash," *Sedalia (MO) Democrat*, June 28, 1931.
313. "Army Plane Noses Over at Municipal Airport Here," *Jefferson City (MO) Post-Tribune*, July 18, 1931.
314. Ibid.
315. "May Open Canning Factory in Airport at Jefferson City," *Moberly (MO) Monitor-Index*, February 23, 1933.
316. "Plans for Air Mail Programs," *Jefferson City (MO) Post-Tribune*, May 5, 1938.
317. Jeremy Amick, "'Mutual Helpfulness' Co-founder of American Legion Post Leaves Legacy of Public Service," War History Online, March 29, 2015.
318. Ibid.
319. Ibid.
320. "Lincoln University," *The Crisis*, December 1940.
321. "Local Pilot Hails Private Flying Valuable to Defense," *Jefferson City (MO) Post Tribune*, November 25, 1940.
322. *New York Age*, October 12, 1940.
323. Cecil Peterson, Cecil Peterson Collection on the Tuskegee Airmen, Special Collections & University Archives, University of California, Riverside.
324. Ibid.
325. Ross Malone, *Missouri's Forgotten Heroes* (N.p.: CreateSpace Independent Publishing, 2016).
326. Daniel Haulman, *The Tuskegee Airmen Chronology* (Montgomery, AL: New South Books, 2018).
327. "Wilber Long Makes First Lincoln U. Solo Flight," undated clipping from Naomi Long Madgett.
328. Erica Smith, "Tuskegee Airmen Held as POWs," *St. Louis Post-Dispatch*, September 26, 2009.
329. "Airport Becomes a Victory Garden," *Moberly (MO) Monitor-Index*, July 13, 1943.

Chapter 12

330. Young, *Pioneers of High, Water and Main*.
331. Ibid.
332. "The Wind Mill." *State Republican* (Jefferson City, MO), May 2, 1895.
333. Ibid.
334. "New Buildings: Fred Knaup's Residence," *State Journal* (Jefferson City, MO), January 4, 1878.
335. Minnie Hahn Boyce, "Her Historical Wardrobe," *Jefferson City (MO) Tribune*, March 9, 1947.
336. Ibid.
337. Lewis Larkin, "Capital City Water Co., Is Providing Purest Product with Maximum Service," *Daily Capital News* (Jefferson City, MO), June 5, 1932.
338. Ford, *History of Jefferson City*, 397.
339. Jake Fisher, "Life in Jefferson City, 1869–1901," Cole County Historical Society, Missouri State Archive vertical files, Jefferson City, Missouri.
340. "Patents Granted," *Clinton (MO) Advocate*, February 11, 1886.
341. "Springfield, Missouri, and Surroundings—1889," Springfield-Green County Library.
342. Loring Bullard, "Source to Tap: A History of Missouri's Public Water Supplies" (Springfield, MO: Watershed Press, 2010).
343. "Completion of the Waterworks," *Daily Advocate* (Clinton), December 7, 1886.
344. Paul W. Johns, "MOzarks Moments: P.B. Perkins and His Grand Businesses," *Christian County Headliner News* (Ozark, MO), 2018.
345. Ibid.
346. Fisher, "Life in Jefferson City."
347. Ibid.
348. *History of Cole, Moniteau, Morgan, Benton*.
349. Johnston, *Illustrated Sketch Book and Directory*.
350. Ibid.
351. Ibid.
352. Jake Fisher, "Life in Jefferson City, 1869–1901," Cole County Historical Society. Missouri State Archive vertical files.
353. Ford, *History of Jefferson City*, 168.
354. *State Republican* (Jefferson City, MO), July 16, 1891.
355. City of Jefferson council minutes.
356. *State Republican* (Jefferson City, MO), November 12, 1891.
357. Ibid.
358. Cynthia J. Chapel, "Shifting History, Shifting Mission, Shifting Identity: The Search for Survival at Lincoln University (Jefferson City, Mo.) 1866–1997" (doctoral thesis, Oklahoma State University, 1997).

359. "Prof. A.L. Reynolds, A.B., Supt. of Industrial School Lincoln Institute," *Professional World* (Columbia, MO), December 25, 1903.
360. "Lincoln Institute Day Is Observed at World's Fair," *St. Louis Globe-Democrat*, July 20, 1904.
361. Larkin, "Capital City Water Co."

Chapter 13

362. "Wm. Griffin First Lamp Lighter of J.C., Dies," *Lincoln Clarion* (Jefferson City, MO), April 5, 1950.
363. "Utilities Merged to Bring Light, Heat, Power to City," *Sunday News and Tribune* (Jefferson City, MO), March 16, 1952.
364. Ibid.
365. "An Ordinance to Provide for Lighting the City of Jefferson with Gas," *Peoples' Tribune* (Jefferson City, MO), December 20, 1871.
366. "Gas Works," *Peoples' Tribune* (Jefferson City, MO), March 27, 1872.
367. "And There Was Light," *Peoples' Tribune* (Jefferson City, MO), October 9, 1872.
368. Ibid.
369. "The Gas Company," *Peoples' Tribune* (Jefferson City), January 3, 1872.
370. *State Journal* (Jefferson City, MO), February 11, 1876.
371. "Good Citizen Dead," *Springfield (MO) News-Leader*, December 9, 1896.
372. "Local News," *State Journal* (Jefferson City), May 14, 1875.
373. "Hedge Grove Cemetery," *Peoples' Tribune* (Jefferson City), January 30, 1878.
374. "And There Was Light."
375. Ford, *History of Jefferson City*.
376. Ibid.
377. "New Corporations," *St. Louis Post-Dispatch*, December 24, 1886.
378. "Hotels" Folder #1624, Cole County Historical Society, Jefferson City, Missouri.
379. "Capital Cutlets," *Sedalia (MO) Weekly Bazoo*, February 26, 1884.
380. "The Dead Executive," *St. Louis Globe-Democrat*, December 30, 1887.
381. *State Republican* (Jefferson City), January 30, 1896.
382. "Mrs. L. Wagner Is Dead After Brief Illness," *Jefferson City Post Tribune*, July 5, 1938.
383. "Ex-Sheriff Held Up," *St. Louis Post-Dispatch*, November 8, 1898.
384. "Popular Jefferson City Belles Win Free Trips to World's Fair," *St. Louis Post-Dispatch*, April 17, 1904.
385. "75 to 150 Years Ago," *Daily Capital News* (Jefferson City, MO), June 10, 1971.

386. Ibid.
387. Ibid.
388. Ibid.
389. "Utilities Merged to Bring Light."
390. Herbert McDougal, "Home of Missouri's Capitol," *St. Joseph (MO) Gazette*, March 15, 1915.
391. "A Contract for Better Light," *State Republican* (Jefferson City, MO), August 20, 1891.
392. Ibid.
393. Ibid.
394. "Proclamation," *State Republican* (Jefferson City, MO), February 25, 1892.
395. "Utilities Merged to Bring Light."
396. Ibid.
397. *State Journal* (Jefferson City, MO), April 21, 1876.
398. Ford, *History of Jefferson City*.
399. "Dodge Coach Draws Favorable Notice," *Daily Capital News* (Jefferson City, MO), February 15, 1925.
400. "Start on Theater in Two Weeks," *Jefferson City (MO) Post Tribune*, January 15, 1935.
401. "Man of Training and Experience," *Jefferson City (MO) Post Tribune*, October 24, 1934.
402. "Former McCarty St. School Is Converted into 8 Apartments," *Sunday News and Tribune* (Jefferson City, MO), May 24, 1936.
403. "Utilities Merged to Bring Light."
404. Ralph Webb, director of Central Missouri Division, Ameren Missouri, interview with author, February 17, 2021.

Chapter 14

405. Urbana Group, "Jefferson City Historic East Architectural/Historic Survey," Jefferson City Commission on Historic Preservation, Jefferson City, Missouri, 1992.
406. Michelle Brooks and Madeleine Leroux, "High Street Viaduct Has History All Its Own," *Jefferson City (MO) News Tribune*, December 19, 2015.
407. "The Old Home Town Has Done a Lot of Growing and More Will Follow Free Bridge and Highway," *Jefferson City (MO) Post Tribune*, August 21, 1929.
408. Nancy Arnold Thompson, "Charles Warren Thomas," Findagrave.com.
409. Brooks and Leroux, "High Street Viaduct."
410. Johnston, *Illustrated Sketch Book and Directory*.
411. Brooks and Leroux, "High Street Viaduct."

412. Ibid.
413. Ibid.
414. Ibid.
415. Ibid.
416. "Committee to Get Ideas in Other Cities," *Daily Capital News* (Jefferson City, MO), May 19, 1925.
417. *Springfield News-Leader*, April 7, 1923.
418. Ibid.
419. "Lutkewitte Recalls Lifetime as Reporter, Editor in Capital City," *Sunday News and Tribune* (Jefferson City, MO), October 7, 1956.
420. "How Streets Are Built and Maintained in City," *Sunday News and Tribune* (Jefferson City, MO), June 9, 1935.
421. Ibid.
422. "City Improvements," *State Journal* (Jefferson City, MO), April 28, 1876.
423. Ibid.
424. Urbana Group, "Jefferson City Historic East."
425. "Jefferson City," *State Republican* (Jefferson City, MO), March 12, 1896.
426. *Historic American Engineering Record*, Creator, and William Armstrong Davison, "Jefferson Street Bridge, Spanning East Branch of Wears Creek," Jefferson City, Cole County, Missouri, Jefferson City Cole County Missouri, 1968.
427. "How Streets Are Built."
428. "Jefferson City's Uptown 50 Years Ago," *Daily Capital News* (Jefferson City, MO), June 30, 1943.

Chapter 15

429. Ford, *History of Jefferson City*, 482.
430. "Capital City Telephone Company 35 Years," *Sunday News and Tribune* (Jefferson City, MO), June 9, 1935.
431. Missouri Telephone Association staff, *The Show Me State Story: The History of Telephony in Missouri* (Jefferson City: Missouri Telephone Association, 1989).
432. "Capital City Telephone Company 35 Years."
433. Missouri Telephone Association staff, *Show Me State Story*.
434. Nancy Ann Hudson, "67 Years of Service: 1900–1967," Jefferson City Chamber of Commerce, Jefferson City, Missouri, 1967.
435. Missouri Telephone Association staff, *Show Me State Story*.
436. Ibid.
437. Hudson, "67 Years of Service."
438. Ford, *History of Jefferson City*, 482.

439. Hudson, "67 Years of Service."
440. Ibid.
441. Ibid.
442. Ibid.
443. Michelle Brooks, "McHenry Family Leaves Landmark Home, Legacy in Capital City," *Jefferson City (MO) News Tribune*, City Landmark series, 2016.
444. *Evening Missourian* (Columbia), January 17, 1919.
445. Brooks, "McHenry Family Leaves Landmark Home."
446. "Former Phone Building Is Entirely New," *Daily Capital News* (Jefferson City, MO), April 26, 1931.
447. Ibid.
448. Ibid.
449. "Houck McHenry Died at Home on Green Berry Age 68," *Daily Capital News* (Jefferson City, MO), October 28, 1936.
450. Hudson, "67 Years of Service."
451. *Jefferson City (MO) Post Tribune*, September 11, 1918.
452. Brooks, "McHenry Family Leaves Landmark Home."
453. "Foster McHenry New Telephone Group President," *Daily Capital News* (Jefferson City, MO), October 16, 1959.
454. "Houck McHenry," National Independent Telecommunications Pioneer Association Hall of Fame.
455. "Foster McHenry Named," *Jefferson City (MO) Post Tribune*, May 1, 1950.
456. Brooks, "McHenry Family Leaves Landmark Home."
457. "McHenry in 49th Year as Head of Phone Company," *Jefferson City (MO) Post Tribune*, January 12, 1949.
458. Hudson, "67 Years of Service."
459. Ibid.
460. "Phone Official Rotary Speaker," *Sunday News and Tribune* (Jefferson City, MO), April 27, 1969.

Chapter 16

461. "Gotleib Martin Died," *People's Tribune* (Jefferson City, MO), March 5, 1873.
462. "Ibid.
463. Brooks, Michelle. "Governor's Mansion Has Been Shaped by History, Personal Touches of Governors," *Jefferson City (MO) News Tribune*, City Landmark series, April 16, 2016.
464. "IOOF Lodge #37 Resolution," *State Journal* (Jefferson City, MO), March 14, 1873.
465. "Hammer and Saw Noise at Bragg Hall," *Jefferson City (MO) People's Tribune*, February 26, 1873.

466. Ford, *History of Jefferson City*, 200.
467. "U.S., Confederate Applications for Presidential Pardons, 1865–1867," National Archives, Ancestry.com.
468. "Sale of the Dunscomb Property," *Peoples' Tribune* (Jefferson City, MO), May 15, 1872.
469. Lawrence Lutkewitte, "When City Hall Was a Four-Story Business Building Housing the Town's Only Theater and How It Was Bequeath to the City," *Daily Capital News* (Jefferson City, MO), April 5, 1931.
470. "Deed of Trust," *Jefferson City (MO) People's Tribune*, October 21, 1874.
471. "The Syndicate Has Taken in the Jefferson Theater at Jefferson City," *Kansas City Star*, July 3, 1910.
472. *Jefferson City (MO) People's Tribune*, October 16, 1878.
473. "The Syndicate Has Taken."
474. "Poor Old Jefferson City," *Sedalia (MO) Weekly Bazoo*, September 22, 1885.
475. Lutkewitte, "When City Hall Was a Four-Story Business Building."
476. "Local News," *State Journal* (Jefferson City, MO), September 10, 1875.
477. Michelle Brooks, "Clarke Legacy Restored in Family Mausoleum," *Jefferson City (MO) News Tribune*, July 10, 2016.
478. "Joseph M. Clarke," Missouri, U.S., Wills and Probate Records, 1766–1988, Cole County, Ancestry.com.
479. Ibid
480. *Daily Capital News* (Jefferson City, MO), May 23, 1929.
481. Ibid.
482. "City Hall Question," *Jefferson City (MO) Post Tribune*, February 8, 1946.
483. "New City Hall Chances Remote," *Sunday News and Tribune* (Jefferson City, MO), January 27, 1974.
484. Brooks, "Clarke Legacy Restored."
485. Lutkewitte, "When City Hall Was a Four-Story Business."
486. Margaret Morris Pinet, "City Hall Is Monument to J.M. Clark, the Builder," *Sunday News and Tribune* (Jefferson City, MO), July 18, 1943.
487. *History of Cole, Moniteau, Morgan, Benton*.
488. Brooks, "Clarke Legacy Restored."
489. "Old Merchant's Bank." Unknown clipping. Nancy Arnold Thompson collection.
490. "Joseph M. Clarke." Missouri, U.S., Wills and Probate Records, www.familysearch.org.
491. Pinet, "City Hall Is Monument."
492. Bob Priddy, "J.M. Clarke History," speech given on June 3, 2011, to First Christian Church.
493. Ibid.
494. Ibid.

Chapter 17

495. Susan K. Appel, "Jefferson City Community Center," National Register of Historic Places Registration Form, URBANA Group for City of Jefferson, 1992.
496. Ibid.
497. William Sherman Savage, *The History of Lincoln University* (Jefferson City, MO: Lincoln University Press, 1939).
498. Ibid.
499. Loretta E. Owens, "Will Dedicate Civic Center," *Lincoln Clarion* (Jefferson City, MO), November 27, 1942.
500. Ibid.
501. Michelle Brooks, "Estella Branham Diggs, a Woman of Faith and Action," *Jefferson City (MO) News Tribune*, October 3, 2020.
502. Ibid.
503. Ibid.
504. Ibid.
505. "To Our Citizens," *Daily Capital News* (Jefferson City, MO), November 20, 1942.
506. "Lions Club Playgrounds to Be Opened Next Tuesday Morning," *Jefferson City (MO) Post Tribune*, May 27, 1938.
507. Owens, "Will Dedicate Civic Center."
508. "To Our Friends," *Daily Capital News* (Jefferson City, MO), December 25, 1942.
509. Owens, "Will Dedicate Civic Center."
510. "Scouts Mark Anniversary," *Lincoln Clarion* (Jefferson City), February 5, 1943.
511. Owens, "Will Dedicate Civic Center."
512. Appel, "Jefferson City Community Center."
513. "Charles Robinson Dies Wednesday," *Daily Capital News* (Jefferson City, MO), August 15, 1974.
514. Michelle Brooks, "'Lefty' Robinson, the King of Jefferson City Mohawk Baseball," *Jefferson City (MO) News Tribune*, November 25, 2019.
515. Ibid.
516. Appel, "Jefferson City Community Center."

Chapter 18

517. Michelle Brooks, Nomination for Parsons House to the Missouri Alliance for Historic Preservation's Places in Peril, unpublished, 2016.

518. Myrene H. Hobbs, "First of Noted Local Family Was Employed by Jefferson at Monticello," *Daily Capital News* (Jefferson City, MO), March 20, 1942.
519. John Bassett Moore, "Mildred Standish v. Mexico #385," *History and Digest of International Arbitration*, 1898, 3004.
520. Deborah Goldammer, research notes, Jefferson City, Missouri.
521. Michelle Brooks, "Parsons House—Home to History," *Jefferson City (MO) News Tribune*, March 15, 2009.
522. "St. Louis, Missouri, Marriage Index, 1804–1876," Ancestry.com.
523. Young, *Pioneers of High, Water and Main*, 68.
524. "Mrs. Standish's Funeral at Grace Church 3:30," *Jefferson City (MO) Daily Capital News*, May 25, 1919.
525. 1860 U.S. Census.
526. Mosby Monroe Parsons Papers, Missouri Historical Society Archives, St. Louis. Folder 11.
527. Ibid.
528. Ibid.
529. Ibid.
530. Ibid.
531. Ibid.
532. "Mrs. Standish's Funeral at Grace Church 3:30," *Jefferson City Daily Capital News*, May 25, 1919.
533. Mosby Monroe Parsons Papers, Missouri Historical Society Archives, St. Louis, Folder 11.
534. Brooks, "Parsons House."
535. "Austin M. Standish," *Jefferson City (MO) Peoples Tribune*, June 24, 1874.
536. Moore, "Mildred Standish v. Mexico #385," 3004.
537. Hobbs, "First of Noted Local Family."
538. Missouri School for the Blind Collection, Missouri State Archive, Jefferson City, Missouri.
539. Ibid.
540. "Richard H. Standish," *St. Joseph (MO) Gazette-Herald*, October 7, 1884.
541. *Jefferson City (MO) Democrat Tribune*, May 24, 1919.
542. "Daughters of the Confederacy," *St. Louis Globe-Democrat*, July 19, 1898.
543. *Jefferson City (MO) Daily Capital News*, March 2, 1919.
544. *Jefferson City (MO) Democrat Tribune*, May 24, 1919.

INDEX

A

Ambrose, Joseph 104, 105, 106
American Legion Toney Jenkins Post 139
Ashe, Malcolm 93, 94

B

Baber, Hiram 20, 24, 26, 27
Barcroft, Elias 15, 16, 27
Bass, Peter 18
Basye, Alfred 19, 20, 24, 25
Basye, Susan 25, 79
Benton, Thomas Hart 46, 78
Bergman, Stephen 31
Berry D'Oench, Nancy 145
Berry, Green C. 143
Binder, Fred 82, 86, 100, 101, 106, 130
Blosser, Bob 61, 62
Bohrer Wagner, Lena 107
Bolton, Lydia 76
Bolton McHenry, Thenia 122, 125
Bolton Price, Celeste 114
Boone, Daniel Morgan 16, 17
Bowman, Cecil 91
Bragg Hall 129, 130, 131, 132
Bragg, Henry 129, 130
Branham Diggs, Estella 137, 138
Bruns Decker, Effie 110
Bruns Hess, Ottillia 109
Buckner, Rev. Xerxes Xavier 104, 105, 106
Burkhardt, Theodore 117

C

Callaway Hills 64
Capital City Planing Company 82
Capitol Hill 13, 23, 34, 70
Carnegie Library 70, 82
Carter, James E. 106, 131
Casey, Christopher 19, 23, 24
Casey, Hardin 23, 24, 69
Cecil Thomas 113
Central Hotel 18, 57

INDEX

Central United Church of Christ 34, 36, 101
Chambers, Joshua 26
Cheney, W.G. 50
Christian Science Church 36
Churchill, British prime minister Winston 88
city hall 95, 127, 129, 132, 133
City Hotel 75, 99, 107
Clarke, Joseph 129, 130, 131, 132, 133, 134, 135
Cole County 7, 9, 10, 11, 13, 15, 17, 20, 22, 24, 25, 26, 27, 28, 30, 32, 37, 40, 50, 51, 64, 71, 72, 80, 82, 86, 92, 123, 124, 129, 142, 155
Cole County Courthouse 18, 22, 25, 26, 95, 100, 131
Cole, Nelson 79, 80
Colgan, Daniel 22, 23
Colgan, Daniel, Jr. 19
College Hill 13, 19, 31, 70
Commercial Club 84, 86, 106, 123, 134
Community Chest 138, 139
Conrow, Aaron 144
Cooper, Roland 139
Cordell, E.B. 70
Corwin, Charlton Jason 50, 51
Corwin, Charly Basye 51
Corwin, Willis Porter 51, 53, 54, 55
Cote sans Dessein 7, 11, 13, 14, 15, 16, 17, 18, 20, 22, 24, 39, 40, 69, 74
Crump, Cassandra 80
Crump, James 35

D

Dalllmeyer, Rudolph 86
Dallmeyer, William 100
Damel, Estella 136, 137
Damel, Prof. John 136
Davison, William 100, 116
Decker, Ernest W., III 109, 110
Diggs, John "Duke" 137, 138
Dorris, Dr. Stephen 20, 23
Dorris, McDaniel 20, 23
Dulle, Gerhard Herman 72
Dulle, Gerhart Herman 32, 33, 34, 109
Dunnica, James 22, 23, 39
Dunnica, William F. 39, 40

E

Edward H. Winter 154
Edwards, E.L. 37, 42, 45, 130
Eveler, Bernard 30, 31
Ewing, H. Clay 73
Ewing, Robert Allen 17, 23
Executive Mansion 22, 23, 34, 43, 44, 100, 108, 116, 129

F

First Christian Church 58, 131, 135
First Presbyterian Church 19, 43, 62
First United Methodist Church 80
Fisher, Jake 100, 106

G

Garnett, Reuben 23, 41
General Assembly 16, 17, 22, 23, 37, 39, 40, 42, 54, 86, 116, 123, 131, 133, 144
Glenn, Charles 70, 71
Goose Bottoms 33, 34, 70, 97, 102, 113

INDEX

Gordon, John C., Jr. 18, 24, 37, 40
Gordon Parker, Zue 122
Gordon, Pemberton 58
Goshorn, Robert C. 38, 50, 57, 59, 60, 61
Governor
  Bakers, Sam A. 55
  Brown, B. Gratz 43, 44, 78
  Caulfield, Henry 90
  Crittenden, Thomas 78
  Edwards, John C. 45
  Hadley, Herbert 101
  Jackson, Claiborne 25
  Majors, Elliott W. 53
  Marmaduke, John 106
  Miller, John 23
  Price, Sterling 46, 78
  Stephens, Lon 79
Grace Episcopal Church 82
Grant, Gen. Ulysses 25, 144
Griffin, William 104
Gundelfinger, William 89
Gunn, Calvin 22, 23, 25, 37, 39, 40, 41, 42, 43, 44, 59, 72

H

Haar, Henry 29
Haar, Herman 31
Hardin Casey 25
Helias, Father Ferdinand 29, 30
Herman, Allen 133
Herman, Robert 133
Hess, Charles 108, 109
Hope, Adam 17, 18

I

Independent Order of Odd Fellows 47, 129

J

Jackson, Mary 80, 81
James A. Garfield GAR Post #6 49
James, Frank 78, 79
Jane Ramsey Ewing 18
Jefferson City Air Field 89, 91, 92, 93, 94
Jefferson City Area Chamber of Commerce 84, 86, 89, 115, 138
Jefferson City Chess Club 105
Jefferson City Community Center 127, 136, 138
Jefferson City Country Club 115
Jefferson City Junior College 92
Jefferson City Mohawks 140
Jefferson City Sand Company 83
John C. Gordon Sr 24
Jones, Robert 15
Jones, William 15, 18

K

Kaiser, J.B. 107
Knaup, Fred 57, 98, 99, 107, 130
Koch, Paul 89
Kolkmeyer, Christopher 34
KRCG 38, 61, 62, 63
Krekel, Alfred 131
Krekel, Arnold 72, 109
Kremer, Gary 73
KWOS 38, 57, 58, 61, 63, 154

L

Lincoln Institute 12, 43, 92, 93, 94, 95, 102, 136, 138, 139
Linkenmeyer, William 117
Linn, Dr. Henry "Duncan" 142

INDEX

Linxwiler Albert 89
Linxwiler, Albert 92
Lions Clubs 138
Lohman, Charles 35
Lohman Opera House 131
Long, Wilbur 94
Lusk, James 46, 47
Lusk, William 42, 46
Lusk, William H., Jr 47, 48, 49
Lutkewitte, Lawrence 9, 61, 64, 73, 115, 133

M

Madison Hotel 107, 122, 130
Magerlee, Philip 32
Marion 13, 14, 15, 19, 24, 26, 41, 46, 69, 75
Martin, Gottlieb 129
Masons 23, 134
Maus, Charles 35, 36
Maus, Christopher 35
Maus, Elisabeth 35
Maus, Frederick 35
Maus, George 35
Maus, Jacob 35
Maus, Killian 35, 36
Mayor
  Bruns, Dr. Bernard 109
  Christy, John 133
  Grimshaw, Arthur 82, 84, 86
  Grimshaw, Jonathan 82, 84, 85
  Jenkins, Earl 132
  Owens, Jesse 139
  Price, Thomas Lawson 70, 74, 75, 76, 101, 114
  Thomas, Cecil 53, 113, 114, 115, 133
McCarty, Burr H. 67, 74, 76, 78
McCarty, Ella 79

McCarty, Ella McCarty 78
McCarty House 78, 79, 80
McHenry, Foster 122, 124, 125
McHenry, Houck 120, 121, 122, 123, 124, 125
McHenry, James 15
McHenry, Jim 124, 125
McHenry, John 124, 125
Merchants Bank 100, 133
Miller, Frank 125, 131
Miller, George 25
Miller, Peter 35
Minor, James L. 17
Missouri Hotel 35
Missouri Pacific Railroad depot 38, 51, 53, 79, 80, 82, 83, 84, 86, 101, 105, 121
Missouri River 8, 9, 13, 15, 16, 22, 23, 24, 27, 67, 69, 70, 73, 74, 75, 82, 83, 86, 87, 89, 90, 95, 97, 107, 114, 119, 141
Missouri State Penitentiary 23, 43, 44, 55, 70, 99, 101, 105, 107, 108, 116, 144
Modern Priscilla Club 137, 138, 139
Monroe House 100, 106, 107, 131
Muessig, Johnny 58
Munichburg 105

N

New Moon Hotel 80

O

Oberman, Theodore 89
Obermayer, Joseph 35
Obermayer, Louis 35
Obermayer, Moritz 35

Index

Obermayer, Simon 35
Oliver Buehrle Chapter #17 of the Disabled American Veterans 124

P

Parker, Lester Shepherd 121, 122
Parsons, Gustavus 141, 142
Parsons, Mosby Monroe 143, 144
Parsons Standish, Mildred 127, 141, 142, 143, 144, 145
Parsons, Stephen "Kearney" 144
Perkins, Paul 99, 100
Porth, Joseph 86, 120
post office 17, 25, 47, 75, 100, 116
Price, Caroline Long 101
Price, Thomas Lawson 113
Pruitt, Wendell 93, 94
public printer 46, 47, 48
Pullam, Richard 93, 94

R

Raithel, Victor 91
Ramsey Ewing, Jane 17
Ramsey, Jonathan 16, 17, 18
Ramsey, Josiah Jr 16, 17, 18, 22, 24, 69
Ramsey, Josiah Jr 17
Randolph, John 92, 93, 94
Read, Israel 40
Regan, James F. 106
Regan, Joseph F. 50, 131
Reynolds, Prof. A.L. 102
Rhyno, Lenore 62
Rising Sun 18, 24, 25, 30, 37, 40, 44, 79
Robertson Aircraft Corporation 91, 92, 94

Roberts, W.B. 120
Robinson, Charles "Lefty," Sr. 139, 140
Rogers, Jefferson T. 23, 67, 69, 70, 71, 72, 73
Roscoe Enloe American Legion Post #5 92, 124
Royston, Jesse Franklin 18, 24
Ruwart, Henry 99

S

Schmidt, Frank 131
Schnitzelbankers 55
Schott, Fritz 57
Schott, John G. 98
Schultz, Otto 57
Second Baptist Church 60
Snodgrass, Harry 55
Standish, Austin 142, 143, 144
St. Louis Cardinals 58
Stokes, Mary 80, 81
St. Peter Church 30, 32, 34, 82, 101
Supreme Court 46, 71, 81, 97, 99, 108, 112, 114

T

Tellman, Herman 34
Temple Beth El 34
Topham Grimshaw, Eliza Maria 85
Truman, Pres. Harry 63, 88
Tweedie, William 89
Tyrrel, Henry 121

V

Virginia Hotel 76

W

Waddill McHenry, Madge 124, 125
Wagner, George 106
Wagner, William 86, 100, 106, 107, 131
Wallau, Henry 82, 83
Wallendorf, Josephi 28, 34
Wallendorf, Mathias 34
Warner, Wyncoop 17, 18
Washington, Hubert 139
Weir's Creek 71, 72, 83, 97, 105, 114, 116
Weldon, Betty 38, 61, 62, 63, 64, 65
Wilke, August 32
Willis Porter Corwin 53
Will Shriver 64, 65
Winter, Edward 50
Winter, Edward H. 59, 60
Witten, J.M. Don 55
Wolters, Bernard 30

Y

Young, Dr. Robert 73, 97, 142
Yount, John 70

About the Author

Michelle Brooks has enjoyed writing since before she could read, pretending to fill pages of notebooks with swirls. In the sixth grade, her book *Pop Goes the Popcorn!* (illustrated by Renessa Bottom Wiggins) won her a trip to a young author's conference. During high school, she provided copy for the local newspaper, the *Carthage Press*, about her school's activities.

Her first published work was a poem in her college English department's annual magazine.

It became apparent that her strength was in nonfiction, and Michelle returned to newspapers, writing for the college newspaper and then for the *Daily Dunklin Democrat* in Kennett, the *Monroe City News* and the *Current Local* in Van Buren.

Her skills improved immensely due to the influence of editors at the *Jefferson City News Tribune*, to which nineteen years' experience with Central Missouri Newspapers Inc. and more than one hundred newspaper industry awards can attest.

The interest in history matured later. Michelle became a student of Jefferson City history when given the historic preservation beat at the *News Tribune*. Her appreciation for the impacts of local history on present-day events grew over the years.

About the Author

Since studying anthropology and history at Lincoln University, Jefferson City, Michelle has worked on larger research projects, including identification of members of the Sixty-Second U.S. Colored Troops, founders of Lincoln University; finding men who attended Lincoln University and served in the U.S. Army Air Corps during World War II as Tuskegee Airmen; and discovering the broad and pioneering career of her grandfather Harry "HAP" Peebles, who was a country music promoter across the Midwest from 1938 to 1993.

This book is her first, and it has been a learning experience.

Her next book with The History Press will be *Lost Jefferson City* in 2022.